Praying
Like Jesus

Praying
Like Jesus

~ ~

*The Lord's Prayer
in a Culture of Prosperity*

James Mulholland

HarperSanFrancisco
A Division of HarperCollins*Publishers*

Scripture references, unless otherwise noted, are from the New International Version.

PRAYING LIKE JESUS: *The Lord's Prayer in a Culture of Prosperity.* Copyright © 2001 by James Mulholland. All rights reserved. Printed in the United States of America. No part of this book may be used or reproduced in any manner whatsoever without written permission except in the case of brief quotations embodied in critical articles and reviews. For information address HarperCollins Publishers, Inc., 10 East 53rd Street, New York, NY 10022.

HarperCollins books may be purchased for educational, business, or sales promotional use. For information please write: Special Markets Department, HarperCollins Publishers, Inc., 10 East 53rd Street, New York, NY 10022.

HarperCollins Web site: http://www.harpercollins.com
HarperCollins®, ❦®, and HarperSanFrancisco™ are trademarks of HarperCollins Publishers, Inc.

FIRST EDITION
Designed by Joseph Rutt

Library of Congress Cataloging-in-Publication Data
ISBN 0–06–001156–4 (cloth)
01 02 03 04 05 ❖/RRD 10 9 8 7 6 5 4 3

To my wife, Angie,
and my best friend, Phil.
Thank you for your love and faith.

CONTENTS

FOREWORD

I first met Jim Mulholland in 1988 at Christian Theological Seminary in Indianapolis. We were standing in line to pay for our textbooks and struck up a conversation. We've been friends ever since. The true measure of a friendship is not determined so much by its length as it is by its depth. Jim and I go deep.

For the past thirteen years, it has been our custom to meet once a week and discuss our upcoming sermons. Jim has strengthened many a weak sermon of mine and prevented several bad ones from seeing the light of day. I am grateful beyond words. But more than that, Jim has a remarkable knack for squeezing a fresh truth from a Bible text dusty with age. He's draped some awfully bare bones with beautiful garments.

In this book on the Lord's Prayer, Jim takes a familiar, even tired, text, blows the dust off, and gives it new life for the twenty-first century. Those of us concerned that the church has lost its way, who mourn the church's sad allegiance to a culture gone wrong, will find much to celebrate in this little book.

I commend it to you with my full enthusiasm, confident that the message Jim brings will bless your life as it has mine.

Philip Gulley
September 2001

Jesus and Jabez

It was a beautiful spring evening. The disciples were relaxing around a campfire. They'd spent the day watching Jesus teach and heal. Now they were trying to figure out what his words meant and how he acted with such power. In the midst of their discussion, Jesus appeared out of the darkness and joined them.

They grew quiet. They knew Jesus had been somewhere praying. He began and ended nearly every day by finding a solitary place and communing with God. Usually he returned to his disciples with some fresh insight, but tonight he sat silently gazing into the fire. On such nights Jesus wanted to answer their questions.

Thomas, who had been waiting for this opportunity, cleared his throat and said, "Lord, teach us how to pray."

Jesus smiled and said, "When you pray, remember to whom you're speaking. Don't say words merely to impress those who might overhear your conversation with God. Instead, find a quiet place where you can be honest with God. Become more interested in hearing from God than being heard by others. Don't forget that a good conversation includes speaking and listening.

"When you pray, remember to whom you're speaking. There's no need to manipulate God with flowery words, magical formulas, or mindless chants. Such methods are always selfish and designed to trick God into doing what you want. The point of prayer is not to get what you want, but to receive what you need. Don't forget that God knows what you need before you do.

"When you pray, remember to whom you're speaking. Pray like this: 'Our Father in heaven, you are good and holy. Let your kingdom come and your will be done. Let it be on earth as it is in heaven. Give us what we need today. Forgive our sins and help us to forgive others as you have forgiven us. Strengthen us in temptation and deliver us from evil.'"

When Jesus had finished there was an uncomfortable silence. The disciples looked at one another in dismay, hoping someone else would ask the obvious question. Thomas noticed the other disciples staring at him. He cleared his throat again and asked, "Lord, are you sure that's how we should pray?"

Jesus said, "Why do you doubt this time, Thomas?"

Thomas said, "Well, Lord, we've all been praying another prayer every morning. We pray: 'Bless me and enlarge my territory. Let your hand be on me, and keep me from harm so I will feel no pain.'"

Jesus frowned. "And you like that prayer better than mine?"

Thomas replied, "Don't get me wrong, Lord. Your prayer is very nice, but we've already memorized that one, and it seems to work."

Jesus, turning to the other disciples, said, "Do you all feel this way?"

Judas answered, "Lord, there has been more money in the common purse since we began praying that prayer."

John added, "Lord, I don't mean to be critical, but outside of Galilee no one knows who you are. It wouldn't hurt if you asked God to enlarge your territory."

Peter jumped in, "And, Lord, I especially like the part about keeping me free from pain."

Jesus was no longer smiling.

He said, "Let me make this clear. If you would be my disciples, you must deny yourselves, take up your cross, and follow me. Judas, when I sent you out, did I tell you to take gold and silver?"

Judas hung his head. "No."

"Did God provide for all your needs?"

"Yes."

Jesus asked, "John, how many times have I said my kingdom is not of this world?"

John looked away. "I don't know. A lot."

"I want you to memorize these words. You might even want to write them down. My kingdom is not of this world."

"Yes, Lord."

Jesus said, "Peter, do you love me?"

"Of course!"

"Do you love me enough to suffer or even die for me? Or are you more interested in living a life free of pain?"

"Lord, you know I would die for you!"

"Peter, you don't even want to pray my prayer."

Then Jesus stood, shook his head in frustration and disappeared back into the night. He had found more reasons to pray. That night many of his disciples slunk off into the darkness. They said to each other, "This is another hard teaching. Who can accept it?"

The next morning Jesus awoke to discover there were only twelve left around the campfire. He asked, "Do you want to leave too?"

Peter answered, "Lord, to whom would we go? You have the words of eternal life."

• • •

This is not what happened two thousand years ago. Unfortunately, it is happening today in thousands of churches and with millions of Christians. The past few months the Christian world has been abuzz over a little book called *The Prayer of Jabez.* It's topped the *New York Times* bestseller list, and even its author, Bruce Wilkinson, has been surprised by its wild popularity. Thousands of Christians are repeating an obscure prayer first uttered by a man named Jabez over three thousand years ago. Many have become convinced his words are the formula for prosperity.

Across America, hundreds of pastors are being pulled aside by excited church members who are saying, "You have to pray this prayer. It's changed my life." Such a testimony is hard to dispute, especially when it is a prayer that includes the requests "bless me, enlarge my territory, keep your hand on me, and keep me from pain." In a materialistic, self-centered culture, such a prayer will always be attractive.

Many pastors will embrace this prayer wholeheartedly. They will incorporate it into worship and preach a sermon series on each phrase. They will give copies of *The Prayer of Jabez* to their entire congregation. They will ignore the warnings of the author that his book was not intended to justify selfishness. They will encourage their church members to begin every morning with this prayer.

Unfortunately, they won't reflect on the dangers of teaching self-centered people to begin each day with the chant, "Bless me!" They won't worry about the compromises inherent in a marriage of prayer and prosperity. They won't consider the consequences of making prayer into a device for getting what we want. In the midst of this frenzy of egotism, they will overlook the obvious—the Prayer of Jabez isn't the prayer Jesus taught us to pray.

Indeed, in significant ways the Prayer of Jabez is counter to the heart of the gospel and the priorities of Jesus. It represents the advancement of self and the resistance to self-denial Jesus confronted in his day and God continues to challenge within Christianity. And, although Mr. Wilkinson has tried to redeem the words of Jabez, he has only succeeded in fanning into flame the embers of a prosperity theology many had hoped was finally dying. He forgot the reason Jesus didn't teach his disciples the Prayer of Jabez.

Jabez got it wrong.

In fairness to Jabez and to the Bible, neither suggest his prayer should be the model for others. This honor is reserved for another short prayer located in the gospels of Matthew and Luke.[1] It is the prayer Jesus taught his disciples to pray. We call this prayer "The Lord's Prayer," though I prefer to call it the Prayer of Jesus. It is the kind of prayer you and I should pray, not necessarily word for word, in unison, on

Sunday morning, but whenever we need to be reminded of our relationship with God and the world.

This book is intended to encourage those who follow Jesus to pray prayers like the one he taught. Such prayers remember to whom they are speaking. They seek God's will rather than God's blessing. They focus not on our needs, but on the needs of the world. Praying such prayers change the world by changing us.

I invite you to reconsider the Prayer of Jesus. I cannot assure you of material blessing. I cannot promise you expanded prosperity, power, and influence. I cannot guarantee you a life free from struggle and pain. Of course, to expect such results is more like magic than prayer. If you are only interested in getting what you want, I have nothing to offer you.

But if you are tired of asking for what does not satisfy, seeking what fails to fill your needs, and knocking at doors that never open, I encourage you to sit quietly and listen to the one who, Peter said, "has the words of eternal life." He does not offer another gimmick or formula. He offers these simple words:

Our Father, who art in heaven,
hallowed be thy name.
Thy kingdom come. Thy will be done,
on earth as it is in heaven.

Give us this day our daily bread.
Forgive us our sins,
as we forgive those who sin against us.
Lead us not into temptation,
but deliver us from evil.
Amen.

---

1. The Prayer of Jesus is located in Matthew 6:9–13 and Luke 11:2–4. Although there are minor variations between the two texts, they include the same essential phrases. Since the prayer is not in the gospel of Mark, it is generally thought to be part of the "Q" materials available to the gospel writers. It was certainly an early component of Christian worship.

ONE

Ⓢ

When You Pray

Nearly everyone I know prays. Some pray at meals, at sunrise, or at bedtime. Others pray in church, synagogue, or mosque. Some pray to Allah, some to Yahweh. Others pray to Mary and the saints. Still others pray only in Jesus' name. Some pray as a daily discipline, and others only in emergencies. Even my friend who claims prayer doesn't work admits to praying when the doctors found a spot on his lung. "What could it hurt?" he said.

Jesus understood the human inclination for prayer. When he taught his disciples how to pray, he began with the words "When you pray." He did not say "If you pray." Jesus assumed everyone would eventually find a reason to pray. He also knew how easily we abuse prayer.

Jesus said, "The good man brings good things out of the good stored up in his heart, and the evil man brings evil things out of the evil stored in his heart. For out of the overflow of his heart his mouth speaks" (Luke 6:45). Prayer is a window to the human heart and mind. The prayers we recite reveal more about us than about God. They often expose our selfishness and our misconceptions about God.

David prayed, "May his days be few; may another take his place of leadership. May his children be fatherless and his wife a widow. May his children be wandering beggars; may they be driven from their ruined homes. May a creditor seize all he has; may strangers plunder the fruits of his labor. May no one extend kindness to him or take pity on his fatherless children" (Ps. 109:8–12). His prayer reveals the depth of his anger and bitterness. It suggests God is one who curses our enemies. Although it may honestly reflect David's feelings and thoughts, it is not a prayer pleasing to God.

A prayer like that of Jabez is certainly a step above David's prayer, but it too reveals more about Jabez than about God. He prayed, "Bless me and enlarge my territory. Let your hand be with me, and keep me from harm so I will be free from pain" (1 Chron. 4:10). What should we assume about a man who uses the word "me" or "my" four times in two sentences? Is his selfishness any more admirable than David's fury? Is his assumption that God plays favorites any more accurate than David's hope in God's wrath? Many prayers seem more interested in God's curses and blessings than in God.

Prayers need to be judged by their motives as much as their words. I once attended a Sunday school class that ended each morning with the prayer, "The Lord watch between me and thee, when we are absent one from another" (Gen. 31:49, KJV). I often wondered if the members of this class realized they were repeating the prayer Laban and Jacob prayed when they feared being stabbed in the back. The motive of their prayer was self-preservation rather than charity.

Prayers motivated by anger, selfishness, or mistrust are not good models. When we pray for others to be cursed, we expose our lack of grace and mercy. When we seek personal blessing, we display our selfishness. When we become convinced certain words or actions will produce certain results, we make prayer into magic. When prayer becomes a means of getting what we want, we make God into a waiter busily scribbling down our order. Such prayers are a serious matter because they betray the deficiencies of our hearts and minds.

David, on one of his better days, prayed, "Search me, O God, and know my heart; test me and know my anxious thoughts. See if there is any offensive way in me, and lead me in the way everlasting" (Ps. 139:23–24). This may be a prayer we should pray before we begin praying. It acknowledges how easily we pray the wrong prayers for the wrong reasons. David was asking God to teach him how to pray properly.

This was what the disciples were seeking when they asked Jesus to teach them how to pray. It was not as if the disciples had never prayed. Devout Jews prayed the Shema twice a day and eighteen other prayers throughout the day. In asking Jesus to teach them how to pray, they were seeking more than another ritual prayer. They were asking about the proper attitude of prayer.

When I was growing up I often heard pastors use the phrase, "Let's be in the attitude of prayer." Although this was probably a nice way of asking a congregation to "shut up so we can pray," it was also an invitation to prepare ourselves to pray properly. What is the proper attitude for prayer?

Sam Walter Foss addressed this question in his poem "The Prayer of Cyrus Brown":

"The proper way for a man to pray,"
Said Deacon Lemuel Keyes,
"And the only proper attitude
Is down upon his knees."

"No, I should say the way to pray,"
Said Reverend Doctor Wise,

"Is standing straight with outstretched arms
And rapt and upturned eyes."

"Oh, no, no, no," said Elder Slow,
"Such posture is too proud:
A man should pray with eyes fast closed
And head contritely bowed."

"It seems to me his hands should be
Austerely clasped in front,
With both thumbs pointing toward the ground,"
Said Reverend Doctor Blunt.

"Las' year I fell in Hodgkin's well
Head first," said Cyrus Brown,
"With both my heels a stickin' up,
My head a-pinting down;

"An' I made prayer right then an' there,
Best prayer I ever said,
The prayingest prayer I ever prayed,
A-standing on my head."

The proper attitude of prayer is far more than a question
of whether we close our eyes, fall on our knees, lift our hands,

or lay on our face. Cyrus Brown exposed the silliness of such arguments. It is not about finding the right words and the correct formula for addressing God. The proper attitude is not a matter of posture or eloquence; it is matter of humility and trust. Do we recognize our utter dependence upon God? Do we trust God to faithfully meet our needs—especially when life has left us at the bottom of a well?

Although there are many poor motives for prayer, Jesus was especially offended by two kinds of prayer: the prayer of self-righteousness and the prayer of self-interest, which he called "praying like the hypocrites" and "praying like the pagans." They display our arrogance and distrust. I know about these prayers because I've prayed them.

The Prayer of Self-Righteousness

I've prayed the prayer of self-righteousness as long as I can remember. As a child I was encouraged to pray before every meal. I would fold my hands, close my eyes, and recite, "God is great. God is good. Let us thank him for this food. Amen." Sometimes I said it so quickly it sounded as if I were speaking in tongues. At night I would pray, "Now I lay me down to sleep. I pray the Lord my soul to keep." I said these prayers to please my mother rather than to communicate with God. Many of our first prayers are prayed to please others.

I grew up in a church that prayed the Lord's Prayer every Sunday. Every week we would pray in unison, reciting the Prayer of Jesus. It was a monotonous chant without passion or thought. I discovered I could say the word "watermelon" repeatedly while the others prayed and no one would even notice. Though I had this prayer memorized, its meaning was lost to me. Many of our first prayers are meaningless.

As a teenager I became a fan of spontaneous prayer. I was good with words and could quickly craft a prayer that impressed those around me. People would comment about my prayers. I began to listen to the prayers of others and borrow their best phrases and sentiments. I learned that those who pray eloquently are seen as good and holy. Though my prayers were beautiful, they were often empty. Many of us, especially those raised in religious homes, have learned to pray the prayer of self-righteousness.

However, the prayer of self-righteousness is not a proper prayer. It is motivated by pride and vanity. When I pray this way I act as if God answers the most impressive prayers. Of course, I'm not really concerned with whether God answers or not. The true purpose of such prayer is to impress people rather than God. This kind of prayer is all about me: Look at me. Listen to me. Be impressed with me.

Jesus called this "praying like the hypocrites" because to pray this way is to perform rather than pray. The word

15

ite" comes from the Greek word for "actor." The prayer of self-righteousness is meaningless and empty. It is offensive because it isn't prayer at all. It is playacting.

Jesus once told a story about two men who went to the Temple to pray. One was essentially a deacon and a Sunday school teacher. His prayer was similar to this: "Oh, God Almighty, Creator of Heaven and Earth, Omnipotent and Holy, thank you that thou hast created in me a pure heart, that thou hast kept me from evil and blessed me above other men. Thank you that thou hast allowed me to give both my spiritual wisdom and my significant donations to the church."

The second man was the ancient equivalent of a drug dealer and a pimp. He huddled in the back row of the balcony where he was hoping no one would notice him. His head was bowed to hide the tears streaming down his cheeks. His prayer was simple: "God, please forgive me."

Jesus concluded, "I tell you that this man, rather than the other, went home justified before God. For everyone who exalts himself will be humbled, and he who humbles himself will be exalted" (Luke 18:14). The first man's prayer wasn't a plea, but a performance. Instead of applauding from the front row, God was sitting in the balcony listening to the whispers of a humbled and honest man.

I remember one of the first times I prayed an honest and humble prayer. I was twenty-three years old, and my wife had told me she didn't love me anymore and wanted a divorce. That day I lay on my face and sobbed out the most honest of prayers. I prayed, "God, save our marriage."

In that moment I was totally focused on God. I was no longer concerned with carefully crafting my words. I had no desire to be seen or heard by anyone other than God. For the first time in my life, I desperately wanted to be heard by God and to hear God. And God spoke. God revealed the sins in my life that had brought my marriage to the brink of destruction. In the months ahead, he would reveal the steps necessary to save it. I discovered prayer is not intended to influence God, but to allow God to influence us.

Far too often we fill the air with noise, convinced God is impressed by our words. In truth, what God is listening to is our hearts. A humble, honest, and heartfelt prayer is never despised. Indeed, this is the kind of prayer God answers. A well-crafted prayer is worthless when our words don't match our hearts.

One Sunday I preached a sermon on our responsibility to the poor. I ended the service with an eloquent prayer asking God to make us his hands. The prayer was so impressive most of the congregation echoed my "Amen." Although my words were beautiful, I soon discovered the deceitfulness of my heart.

As the last parishioner was shaking my hand at the door, a young woman walked up to the church. She hesitantly asked if I could help her with some food. I wish I could tell you my first reaction was to celebrate how God had answered my prayer. In truth, I had already forgotten my words. I was thinking about the dinner my wife was preparing and looking forward to an afternoon of relaxation.

The young woman's eyes filled with tears as she told me her children were hungry. Guilt, rather than compassion, compelled me to find her some food. As she prepared to leave, she said, "You are really an answer to prayer."

Only then did I remember the eloquent, but empty, prayer I had prayed. I realized we had both been praying that morning. My prayer had been a prayer of self-righteousness, and her prayer had been humble and heartfelt. She had been seeking God while I sought to impress. She had hoped for an answer while I had expected none.

My prayers of self-righteousness always ended with "Amen." Once I had impressed God and anyone else who would listen, my work was done. I had received my reward. There was no need to listen for God's reply. Prayer was a one-way conversation. It was only when I was exposed as a fraud—when I was broken or confronted with my pride— that I heard the voice of God. Once I heard his voice, I became more interested in what God had to say to me than what I could say to God.

The Prayer of Self-Interest

The prayer of self-righteousness was not the only kind of prayer I had to abandon. I had also prayed the prayer of self-interest most of my life. No one had to teach me this prayer. It came naturally. As a child, I would pray for toys. "Dear God, give me a G.I. Joe and roller skates." In December, I addressed my requests to Santa Claus; the rest of the year I petitioned God. My parents tried to teach me to pray for needs rather than wants and to remember the needs of others as well as my own. They would remind me not to pray selfish prayers.

You can imagine my surprise when as a young adult I began to hear some Christian preachers suggest my parents were wrong. These preachers sanctified self-interest and anointed avarice. They encouraged people to pray for toys. Only now the toys were bigger houses, more expensive cars, and larger stock portfolios.

Their message was seductive. It clothed itself in religious platitudes. "You're a child of the King, so you deserve to live like a prince." "God wants you healthy and wealthy." "God blesses those he loves." It defended its legitimacy with Scripture. "Delight yourself in the Lord and he will give you the desires of your heart" (Ps. 37:4). "Ask and it will be given to you" (Matt. 7:7). "You may ask me for anything in my name, and I will do it" (John 14:14). If the desire of your heart was a red Corvette, then all you need do is claim it in Jesus' name and it was yours. Prayer was a means of prosperity.

However, the prayer of self-interest is not a proper prayer. It is motivated by greed. When I pray this way, I act as if God gives only to those who know the magic words. My real concern is how to get God to give me what I want. My desire is to manipulate God rather than to know him. This prayer is about me: Bless me. Protect me. Take care of me.

Jesus called this "praying like the pagans" because to pray this way is idolatry. Idolatry is putting anything before God. The prayer of self-interest is more interested in getting God's blessings than in discerning God's will. It is offensive because it isn't prayer at all. It is manipulation.

Most of us yearn for some magical, mystical means of assuring our blessing and protection. How can we influence or manipulate those forces, divine or otherwise, that alter human destiny? Our attempts can be as simple as carrying a rabbit's foot or wearing a St. Christopher's medal. They can be as elaborate as reading tarot cards or praying the Prayer of Jabez every morning. Superstition and religion have far more in common than we'd like to admit.

Seeking blessing and protection is not a recent phenomenon. We experience a world of natural disasters, disease, famine, and death and conclude that, if there is someone in charge, they are not pleased. How do we please them? How do we earn their blessing and protection? Every culture has attempted to influence those forces beyond human control. We call our culture's attempts "religion" and the attempts of other cultures "superstition."

Although the ways we approach divinity vary, most religions share the assumption that God (or the gods) is hostile and must be appeased. God's favor comes at a price. Divine blessing and protection require the proper offerings. Primitive cultures lay handcrafted tokens or gifts of food and drink before crudely carved idols. When Christians ridicule such attempts, we forget our own history and theology. Judaism was centered around feasts in which thousands of birds and animals were sacrificed on altars. Christianity claims Jesus' death was necessary to satisfy the wrath of God and provide forgiveness and favor to those "washed in his blood." The image of God demanding a sacrifice as a condition of favor persists.

Although we may have advanced beyond the days of sacrificing animals (and sometimes people), many continue to fear God's wrath and seek ways to earn God's blessing. We remain convinced there is a secret formula for pleasing God. If we can find it, we will prosper and be protected. For many, prayer is simply another attempt to appease and manipulate

God. We are too sophisticated to offer God bloody sacrifices or material gifts. Instead, we seek a prayer that will please God and assure our blessing. In so doing, we reduce prayer to an act of self-interest.

This is not a new problem. The prophets of Israel repeatedly condemned manipulative words offered as prayer. Isaiah pronounced God's judgment on such prayers:

> *The multitude of your sacrifices—what are they to me? I have more than enough of burnt offerings, of rams and fat of fattened animals. I have no pleasure in the blood of bulls and lambs and goats. Stop bringing meaningless offerings! Your incense is detestable to me. New Moons, Sabbaths, and convocations—I cannot bear your evil assemblies. When you spread out your hands in prayer, I will hide my eyes from you; even if you offer many prayers, I will not listen. (Isa. 1:11, 13, 15)*

Jesus confronted the same issue in his day. A few days before his death, he entered the Temple in Jerusalem and drove out those selling the birds and animals for sacrifice. He said, "It is written, 'My house will be called a house of prayer,' but you are making it a 'den of robbers'" (Matt. 21:13). This doesn't mean people weren't praying at the Temple. There were probably hundreds of prayers spoken every day. Jesus was upset that the lust for prosperity had obscured the true purpose of prayer and worship.

This distortion of religion continues today. Many preach a gospel of prosperity in which praying certain prayers and claiming certain promises guarantee affluence. They twist the scriptures that promise God's provision into pledges of special favor and blessing. These persons promise health, happiness, and material blessing to those who will give to their ministries. They claim that the more you give them, the more you will receive. They often justify their own wealth and extravagance as evidence of God's preference. They seem convinced a person can serve two masters—money and God.

Like most Christians, I have been able to resist these more blatant prayers of self-interest. I am quickly suspicious of ministers adorned in jewelry and preaching a magical formula for blessing from golden pulpits. I keep remembering that Jesus said, "Be on your guard against all kinds of greed; a man's life does not consist in the abundance of his possessions" (Luke 12:15). Religious greed is merely another kind of greed.

What were more painful to abandon were my prayers for a little more. This was especially difficult in a culture in which success and happiness are measured by an abundance of possessions. Howard Hughes was asked how much

enough. He answered, "One dollar more." It was
to convince myself that what I wanted was what I
needed. It was comfortable for my needs to increase in
direct proportion to my income. It was tempting to focus
my prayers on me.

My prayers of self-interest, like my prayers of self-
righteousness, ended with "Amen." Once I had made my
requests and demands known, the conversation was over. It
never occurred to me that God's answer might be "no." Or
that God might want me to deny my desires and sacrifice
myself in order to accomplish some greater good. I asked for
baubles while God offered a kingdom. It was only when my
selfishness was stripped of its pious trappings—when I realized material possessions would not satisfy or I was confronted with my greed—that I heard the voice of God. Once
I heard his voice, I became more interested in the will of God
than in my own desires.

The prayer of self-righteousness and the prayer of self-
interest share a common theme. They are all about me. They
are self-centered rather than God-focused. They are improper
prayers. The proper attitude for prayer is not playacting or
manipulation. It is bringing our fears, concerns, worries, and
questions to One who has the answers. The point of prayer is
not to tell God what we want, but to receive what we need.
It is not approaching God with our demands, but listening

for God's leading. It is not seeking our will, but learning to discern God's will. This is so important to understand in a culture that caters to our every whim. Prayer isn't about me—it is about God.

Praying Properly

After Jesus finished telling his disciples how not to pray, he shared a model prayer with them. He said, "Pray like this." Notice he did not tell them to pray his exact words. After all, he had just warned them not to grandstand like the hypocrites or babble on like the pagans. What he was suggesting was a pattern to prayer that included the ingredients for a healthy and satisfying relationship with God and the world. Jesus was encouraging us to pray like him.

Praying like Jesus offers far more than prosperity. When prayed with sincerity, it cleanses our hearts of self-righteousness and strips our motives of self-interest. It challenges the false and inappropriate ways we approach God and each other. It reminds us of what we so easily forget—our proper relationship to God and the world.

Praying like Jesus reminds us to whom we are speaking. God is not hostile. Prayer is not persuading an indifferent Lord, or manipulating an obstinate Master, or lobbying a reluctant Ruler, or pleading with a stingy Boss. Prayer is climbing into

a Parent who knows what we need before we ask.
is and can be trusted to meet our needs.

Praying like Jesus reminds us of our responsibility as children of God. God is not distant. God is at work in the world. Prayer is not listing our complaints, requests, and demands. Prayer is setting those lists aside and humbly seeking ways to establish God's kingdom and do God's will, on earth as it is in heaven. It is a pledge rather than a petition.

Praying like Jesus reminds us that we are brothers and sisters. God created and loves us all. God is equally concerned for every person. Prayer is not trying to get a bigger piece of the pie. Prayer is an opportunity for God to teach us how to love and live unselfishly. We are blessed in order to be a blessing.

Praying like Jesus reminds us of our need to be forgiven and to offer forgiveness. God offers and expects grace. When prayer fails to acknowledge our sin and to seek to forgive others, then we have forgotten the greatest obstacle to healthy relationship. Prayer longs to restore our proper relationship with God and everyone else.

Finally, Praying like Jesus reminds us of the temptation to trust in riches and depend on material blessing. The children of God need not seek security in stocks and bonds. Our treasure is in heaven. Prayer acknowledges our dependence upon God and our need for deliverance from the seduction of silver and the greed for gold.

Praying like Jesus is a commitment to a new way of living. His prayer is to life as a wedding vow is to marriage. It is not the end of the journey, but the beginning. It is falling in love with the one Jesus called "Father."

TWO

◠ ◡

Our Father

Our Father, who art in heaven, hallowed be thy name.

When my brother was five years old, he got separated from my mother in a grocery store. One minute he was at her side. The next, he was alone in an aisle with shelves towering above him and strangers all around him. My mother didn't realize he was lost until she heard his quivering voice calling out, "Helen, Helen!"

My mother quickly found him, hugged him, and wiped away his tears. Then she asked, "Why did you call me Helen?"

My brother replied, "I knew there were lots of mommies here, but I thought there would only be one Helen."

When we pray we face the same challenge my brother faced in that grocery store. There are lots of gods in this world. Nearly every tribe and nation has claimed to know and worship some god. Allah, Vishnu, Baal, Thor, and Zeus are just a few of the names. It's never safe to assume when you and another person are talking about God that you are referring to the same god. If knowing God's name is helpful for theological discussion, it is vital for prayer. What name should we call when we feel lost and afraid?

The Bible struggles with this question. The term for God in Scripture is *Elohim.* This was a generic name for God and was probably the term used by Abraham, Isaac, and Jacob. Indeed, the Bible often defines God as the God (Elohim) of Abraham, Isaac, and Jacob. But Elohim was not God's name. Indeed, Jacob wrestled with Elohim and demanded to know his name. He received God's blessing, but not his name (Gen. 32:22–30).

Moses is credited with learning the name of the God of Abraham, Isaac, and Jacob. At the burning bush, God (Elohim) commands Moses to return to Egypt and free the people of Israel from slavery. Moses, suspicious this voice might not be God, says, "Suppose I go to the Israelites and say to them, 'The God of your fathers has sent me to you' and they ask me, 'What is his name?' Then what shall I tell them?" (Exod. 3:13).

God responds, "Say to the Israelites, 'The Lord *(Yahweh),* the God (Elohim) of your fathers—the God of Abraham, the God of Isaac, and God of Jacob—has sent me to you.' This is my name forever, the name by which I am to be remembered from generation to generation" (v. 15). The God of Israel is Yahweh.

Of course, Yahweh may not be the proper pronunciation. The Hebrew Scriptures did not include vowels and Yahweh was written as: YHWH. When Jews encountered these letters in Scripture they would use the word *Adonai,* which translates as "Lord." They believed Yahweh to be the name of God, but they discouraged people from speaking it because it was thought too holy to utter.

The God of Israel was hidden in a cloud and shrouded by a curtain. He was Lord and King, enthroned in heaven, awesome and holy. To see his face was to risk death. Those who petitioned him came on bent knee. They prefaced their prayers with acknowledgments of God's power and glory. They sought to appease his anger and earn his favor.

In the midst of such fearsome and majestic images of God, Jesus taught his disciples to address God as a parent. Though the Hebrew Scriptures occasionally spoke of God as a father, Jesus claimed that intimacy as his primary image of God. Though they called God, "Wonderful Counselor, Mighty God, Prince of Peace," Jesus was partial to "Everlasting Father" (Isa. 9:6). He refused to allow us to distance God with titles like King and Lord. He threw open the doors of the throne room and invited us in.

arclay told the story of an emperor riding
at the head of his legions. His son, excited to
...ther, burrowed through the crowd and under the
legs of a guard in order to run to his father's chariot. The
guard scooped him up and said, "Don't you know who that
is in the chariot? That's the emperor." The boy replied, "He
may be your emperor, but he's my father."[1] Jesus shared the
confidence of the emperor's son. He knew the God so many
had perceived from afar with fear and trembling was a father.

The Prayer of Intimacy

Approaching a king is a very complicated process. You have
to request an audience. You dress to impress and choose the
proper gift. You need to acknowledge the king's titles and
honors. When you approach the throne, you kneel or bow.
You make your requests hoping to earn the king's favor.

People have often approached God in prayer with the
same deference. Often using sacrifices, candles, incense, and
altars, they hoped to influence God's attitude with adoration. God was addressed on bent knee or with head bowed.
No one dared run to the throne of God, jump in his lap, and
call him "Daddy."

Yet this is precisely what Jesus taught. He did not tell his
disciples to pray to Elohim, Yahweh, or even Adonai. He did

not complicate prayer with additional requirements and expectations. He did not suggest God listened to those prayers that were the most flattering. Jesus cut through the confusion and eliminated the pretense. He taught them a prayer of intimacy. He told them when they were lost and afraid to call out to their "Daddy."

This was radical theology. It still is. A few years ago, I was praying in worship when I addressed God as "Daddy." Afterward, Betty, one of the older women of the church, pulled me aside and scolded me for using that intimacy. I explained I was simply calling God by the name Jesus used. Jesus called God *Abba,* a word that translates best as "Daddy." She glared at me and said, "Well, you're not Jesus."

It does seem presumptuous and arrogant to call the creator of the universe your daddy. The religious leaders of Jesus' day were no less offended by his use of the word Abba. In a culture that wouldn't even speak God's name, calling God Abba was nearly blasphemy. Indeed, taking such liberties was one of the reasons Jesus was crucified.

Betty was right in reminding me that I am not Jesus. Sometimes I need that reminder. But she was wrong to scold me for calling God "Daddy." I was simply doing what Jesus encouraged. The God (Elohim) of Jesus is a father (Abba).

You can imagine the tongue-lashing I received a few months later when I suggested it was also appropriate to call

God "Our Mother." I suspect this is precisely the language Jesus would choose today. He used father imagery to counteract those titles that kept God distant and impersonal. In our society, where nearly 50 percent of all children grow up without a father active in their lives, Jesus would probably call God "Our Mother."

Those who vehemently argue for the title "God the Father" miss the point. Jesus was not interested in replacing one rigid title with another. He was defining our relationship to God in a new way. Claiming God as a parent was far more than sentimental fantasy. In so doing, Jesus was challenging how we perceive God. For Jesus, God was the father we cry out for when we awake in the darkness, in the grip of a nightmare. God was the mother who dries our tears and kisses away our pain when we fall and skin our knee. God was a parent—intimate, loving, and committed.

Although the image of a father is a positive one for me, I realize that, in a culture where fathers have often been distant and abusive, identifying God as a father is not always greeted with enthusiasm. However, when I've counseled people with such horrific backgrounds, I've discovered they have a very clear sense of what a good parent should be. They know the intimacy they needed and missed.

It really doesn't matter whether we pray to a father or a mother. Since God is neither male nor female, neither term completely describes God. What concerned Jesus was not God's gender, but any image that denied God's intimate knowledge and concern for his children. He told of a father who gives good gifts to his children, who knows the number of hairs on their heads, who dresses them more splendidly than the flowers of the field, and feeds them more faithfully than he feeds the birds of the air. The father Jesus spoke of was not a stern and distant taskmaster whipping the world into shape. He was a devoted, attentive parent.

Whenever the church emphasizes any image that contradicts the parental affection and commitment of God, it slanders God's character. When we portray God as an angry judge, we make God an abusive parent. When we suggest God is distant and demanding, we divorce God from his children. When we reinforce people's fears about God, we deny our Father's unlimited patience and grace.

Whenever I forget to whom I am speaking, my prayers become selfish and manipulative. How do I get the King to give me what I want? How do I influence the Judge to rule in my favor? How do I get God to be interested in me? Remembering that God is a parent changes the way I pray. I can approach God with confidence in his desire and ability to meet my needs. I can trust him to do what is best for me.

Jesus assured us of God's unfailing love. He said, "Which of you, if his son asks for bread, will give him a stone? Or if he asks for a fish, will give him a snake? If you, then, who are evil, know how to give good gifts to your children, how much more will your Father in heaven give good gifts to those who ask him" (Matt. 7:9–11). God will never hand us a stone or a snake. Indeed, God knows and supplies what we need even when we do not ask.

When I come before God with my complaints and demands, when I ask for what I think will satisfy, seek what I hope will fill my void, and knock at doors I want opened, I am like a distrustful child. In those moments, my Father in heaven scoops me into his arms and says, "Peace. Be still. Trust me." When I finally quiet myself and relax in his presence, I discover my complaints were selfish and my demands unnecessary. I am provided with exactly what I need—his love. I also discover I want to be like him.

The Prayer of Responsibility

One day, after we had visited with my grandfather, I heard my father comment to my mother, "I hope I can be as good a man as my father." Sitting in the backseat of our car, I thought, "I want to be as good a man as my dad." A good parent is always an attractive model for their children. Paul wrote, "Be imitators of God, therefore, as dearly loved children and live a life of love" (Eph. 5:1). Whenever I claim God

as father, I also accept the responsibility to be
taught his disciples to pray with intimacy and

I grew up in a small town where every
grandfather, Spencer, and my father, Royal.
advantage when I walked into the bank as a young man and
asked for a loan. The bank officer looked at my long hair and
torn jeans with obvious suspicion. But when I told him my
name, he smiled and said, "You must be Spencer's grandson
and Royal's boy. I think we can help you." He gave me the
amount I requested without any further question.

Of course, if I had profaned that blessing and defaulted on
the loan, I would have abused my relationship with my
father and grandfather. I would have dishonored our family.
When those of us who are blessed by God fail to imitate his
character and compassion, we dishonor God. Clarence Jordan
said, "You don't take the name of Lord in vain with your lips.
You take it in vain with your life. It isn't the people outside
the church who take God's name in vain. It's the people on
the inside, the nice people who would never dare let one little
cuss word fall off their lips—they're the ones many times
whose lives are totally unchanged by the grace of God."[2]
When we have the audacity to pray "Our Father," we must
also have the courage to live as his children.

I remember occasions when I was tempted to do something I knew was wrong. In those moments, I was restrained

by the thought, "I don't want to bring any shame or embarrassment to my grandfather or to my father." What I wanted most was for people to see the good things I was doing and to tell my grandfather or father, "I saw your boy the other day." I wanted nothing more than to make them proud.

What makes God proud? It isn't rigid compliance with religious rules and ordinances. Jesus was critical of those "who strain out gnats and swallow camels." It isn't magnificent religious rituals and ceremonies. Jesus spent more time eating with sinners than sacrificing at the Temple. It isn't religious organization and efficiency. Jesus collected a ragtag group of religious "nobodies" and societal rejects. What makes God proud is when his children begin to value relationships more than religion.

One day, Jesus was asked to name the greatest commandment. He answered, "'Love the Lord your God with all your heart and with all your soul and with all your mind.' This is the first and greatest commandment" (Matt. 22:37–38). Intimacy with God should be our greatest desire. Without this intimacy, we are left to live for ourselves alone.

Then Jesus added, "The second (commandment) is like it; 'Love your neighbor as yourself'" (Matt. 22:39). In so doing, Jesus moved us from intimacy to responsibility. The primary responsibility of the children of God is to love their neighbors. What pleases God is when his children live in community, relating in peace and sharing in resources. He wants to see his kingdom come and his will be done, on earth as it is in heaven.

We know what this should look like. Isaiah, critical of Israel's infatuation with religious formality, said, "Is not this the kind of fasting I have chosen: to loose the chains of injustice and untie the cords of the yoke, to set the oppressed free and break every yoke? Is it not to share your food with the hungry and to provide the poor wanderer with shelter—when you see the naked, to clothe them, and not turn away your own flesh and blood?" (Isa. 58:6–7).

Who is my neighbor? Who is my flesh and blood? Anyone who can call God "Father," must also be my brother and sister. God is not "my father" alone. God is not the father of "my little group." When I approach God in this way, I betray my self-centeredness. Jesus taught his disciples a prayer of intimacy, responsibility, and community.

The Prayer of Community

When my children were small, they got into an argument. My daughter said, "He's my daddy!" My son angrily responded, "No, he's my daddy!" They argued back and forth until they both began to cry. I finally took them in my arms and said, "I can be daddy to both of you." Unfortunately, dults can be as selfish about God as my children were about me. We want God to be "my daddy."

It was no accident Jesus began his prayer with the words "Our Father" rather than "My Father." This was a crucial distinction. I am reminded of how important every time I use the terms "my car," "my house," or "my children" in the presence of my wife. She is quick to remind me that it is "our car" and "our house." And, when it's three o'clock in the morning and one of the children is throwing up in their room, she reminds me they are "our children."

My inclination is to focus on "my world" rather than God's world. This tendency results in prayer that dwells on my needs, my problems, and my desires. Thomas Merton warned, "To consider persons and events and situations only in light of their effect upon myself is to live on the doorstep of hell."[3] Praying to "Our Father" reminds me that I live in community.

I always listen carefully when the church meets to pray. Often prayer meetings are characterized by selfishness. We pray for our needs and the concerns of those we love. Once, at the end of a series of requests for healing, jobs, and housing, someone prayed for the thousands killed and millions homeless because of an earthquake in India. I was ashamed I hadn't thought to pray for them. Too often I limit my prayers and concern to my family, my church, or my country.

I wonder if it offends God when I ask him to bless and neglect to seek his favor for Africa.

When I begin to pray for those beyond my doorstep, then I begin to pray for heaven on earth. I am reminded that God, like any good father, doesn't play favorites. I can quit maneuvering for better position on his lap. I can stop acting as if God's love for others will diminish his love for me. I can relish my relationship with God without ignoring my responsibility to my brothers and sisters.

Jesus said, "God causes his sun to rise on the evil and the good, and sends rain on the righteous and the unrighteous" (Matt. 5:45). This was good news in a culture where it was thought the rich were favored and the poor were cursed, where they assumed God blessed the righteous and rejected the wicked. If God is interested in all of his children, then I cannot ignore them. If God is our father, then I have millions of brothers and sisters.

When I am reminded to pray for their needs, I am transformed. I often discover my needs are not as serious as I thought. When I pray for the woman dying of cancer, my cold doesn't seem such a burden. When I pray for those dying of starvation in Sudan, my desire for a new house seems selfish. Praying for the needs of others always helps me see how my blessings exceed my needs.

Once, when I was visiting a woman after serious surgery, I was reminded of how powerfully this focus on the needs of others brings healing to us. The woman I visited enjoyed my attention and thanked me for coming. When I asked if I could pray with her, she hesitated. She whispered, "Could you pray for me and the woman in the other bed? She's very ill and no one has come to visit her." So we pulled back the curtain and invited her roommate to pray with us. I suspect my parishioner's quick recovery was aided by her outward focus.

On another occasion, I was preaching in a jail. As part of the service, we asked the men to share their prayer requests. They mentioned their families, their cases, and their struggles. I closed this time by asking them to pray for a young girl in our church who was seriously ill. At the end of the service a man stood with tears in his eyes and said, "Thank you for asking us to pray for that little girl. It made me realize you believe God hears the prayers of a criminal. It also made me remember how blessed I am." Praying to "Our Father" for the needs of our brothers and sisters saves us from selfish prayers.

There is another reason we need to focus on the needs of others. Praying for others reminds me I am often the answer to their need. Being the oldest child in my family, I can remember many times when I would yell, "Mom, Bill can't tie his shoes" or "Dad, Paul needs someone to cut up his meat." They would almost always reply, "You do it for him." When we pray to "Our Father," we ~~are inviting~~ God to tell us how to love ~~one another~~.

Rabbi Hillel posed the question, "If not you, then who? If not now, then when?" Too often we offer our prayers instead of our actions. James admonished the church with these words: "What good is it, my brothers, if a man claims to have faith but has no deeds? Can such faith save him? Suppose a brother or sister is without clothes and daily food. If one of you says to him, 'Go, I wish you well; keep warm and well fed,' but does nothing about his physical needs, what good is it?" (James 2:14–16). Praying to "Our Father" for the needs of our brothers and sisters should create a desire to be part of the answer.

My friend Beth understood this responsibility. She was a member of the board of an inner-city community center. The center needed a new van for transporting the many children in its programs. Beth had been praying that God would supply the funds necessary for purchasing the van. At about the same time, she and her husband were shopping for a new car to replace their older model. One day, it occurred to her that if they kept the car they had, they could donate the money necessary to buy the van.

Her desire to be in community and her willingness to deny herself made it possible for many others to be blessed.

My sadness is how seldom we follow her example. It is so easy to seek intimacy with God while ignoring the call to responsibility and community. Yet when I become aware of the needs of others, I should also recognize my need for self-denial.

The Prayer of Self-Denial

When I was a teenager, my father bought my younger brother a motorcycle. It was an extravagant gift, and I was jealous of my father's apparent favoritism. When I complained to my father, he pulled me aside, and said, "Your brother is having a difficult time right now. I needed to give him that motorcycle as a sign of my love. I need you to trust that I love you as much as I love him."

Many contemporary theologians have argued for God's preferential concern for the poor.[4] In a world with such vast disparities between the "haves" and "have-nots," such a preference is not a sign of favoritism, but an indication of love. It does not mean God loves the poor more than the rich. It means that where there is the greatest need, God has the greatest concern. God's wants prosperity for the poor and self-denial for the rich. Each group has a need. The poor need to have food, shelter, and clothing. The rich need to be stripped of their dependence on the abundance of their possessions. The connection between my wealth and the poverty of others ties our prayers together. The prayer of the poor for what they need should produce the prayer of self-denial from those who are blessed.

One day Jesus met a rich young ruler. He asked, "Teacher, what good thing must I do to get eternal life?" (Matt. 19:16). Jesus did not demand he call him Savior. He did not ask him to repeat a set of spiritual vows. He did not encourage the man's attempts at religious purity.

Jesus said, "Go, sell your possessions and give to the poor, and you will have treasure in heaven. Then come, follow me" (Matt. 19:21). I have heard many sermons explaining why this command applies only to those who need to be freed from their obsession with wealth. But if this story isn't aimed at us, I'm not sure who it targets. No wonder we've reinterpreted the story.

Jesus promised eternal life when the rich man sold his possessions, but we have made salvation an abstraction. It is about right belief or right ritual. We have disconnected a proper relationship with God from self-denial. Yet Zacchaeus, another rich man confronted by Jesus, announced, "Here and now I give half of my possessions to the poor, and if I have cheated anybody out of anything, I will pay back four times the amount." Jesus said to him, "Today salvation has come to this house" (Luke 19:8–9). Self-denial and generosity are evidence that we know God, we recognize our responsibility to be like him, and we seek every opportunity to care for our brothers and sisters.

Jesus said, "If anyone would come after me, he must deny himself and take up his cross daily and follow me" (Luke 9:23). The use of cross imagery is remarkable. Jesus believed his suffering on the cross would have a redemptive impact on the world. When Jesus asks us to deny ourselves and take up a cross, he is asking us to suffer in order to bring healing to a hurting world. Dietrich Bonhoeffer called this "the cost of discipleship."[5]

Following Jesus will only cease to hurt when the pains of the world end. When we seek a painless relationship with God, we must completely ignore our neighbors. Ironically, when we seek such comfort, God does all in his power to move us from complacency and make us aware of our responsibility. The Holy Spirit "guides us into all truth." The truth is that self-denial is an indication that we have become intimate with God.

We are praying like Jesus when we begin calling God "Our Father." These words invite intimacy, responsibility, community, and self-denial. They are the framework for everything else Jesus encourages us to pray. "Thy kingdom come. Thy will be done on earth as it is in heaven" is the obvious response of someone praying "Our Father." Once we know such intimacy, we desire what God desires. Once we accept our responsibility, we share God's love for all his children. Once we understand God's call to community, we commit ourselves to establishing his kingdom. Once we know all of these things, we are willing to deny ourselves in order to see God's will done.

1. William Barclay, *The Gospel of Matthew* (Westminster Press, 1975), p. 203. Barclay has a wonderful discussion of the Prayer of Jesus, with many fine insights.

2. Clarence Jordan, *The Substance of Faith* (Association Press, 1972), p. 135. This is a powerful collection of sermons. His book *Sermon on the Mount* is another good source of insights into the Prayer of Jesus.

3. Thomas Merton, *No Man Is an Island* (Harvest/Harcourt Brace Jovanovich, 1955), p. 24. This book of essays is full of wisdom. This quote comes from his essay "Conscience, Freedom and Prayer."

4. This theme runs throughout the Bible and throughout historic and modern theology. Gustavo Gutiérrez's *A Theology of Liberation* (Orbis Books, 1973) is considered the best modern exposition. Juan Luis Segundo, Walter Brueggemann, John Howard Yoder, and Robert McAfee Brown have all written on this theme. Leonardo Boff's *The Lord's Prayer: The Prayer of Integral Liberation* (Orbis Books, 1983) makes this argument using the Prayer of Jesus.

5. Dietrich Bonhoeffer, *The Cost of Discipleship* (SCM Press, 1959). This classic challenges shallow theology and lukewarm Christianity. It is even more powerful because of the cost Bonhoeffer paid for his Christian witness. (He was murdered by Hitler in the closing days of World War II.) This book includes another wonderful discussion of the Prayer of Jesus.

~ ~

THREE

Thy Kingdom Come

Thy kingdom come.
Thy will be done, on earth as it is in heaven.

Carolyn sat down in my office and said, "I need to know God's will for my life. I have a job offer that would mean more money, more vacation, and less stress, but I would have to work every other Sunday. What should I do?"

As a young pastor I was flattered anyone would value my opinion, and I was quick to offer my advice. Unfortunately, I often discovered that same person back in my office a few weeks or months later demanding to know why God and I had got it wrong. I soon gave up my role as religious psychic. I also decided seeking God's will is quite different from reading a horoscope.

I am always glad when anyone begins to seriously seek the will of God. This is a sign of spiritual maturity. Unfortunately, we often bring the same selfish tendencies to discerning God's will. We make seeking God's will into another selfish act. What does God want me to do? What is his perfect path for me? How can I assure my happiness and success? Some even define God's will as giving health, wealth, and ease to his favorites.

More often, people approach the will of God with fear. We act as if God has his hands behind his back and we must determine which hand holds blessing and which holds wrath. We assume God's will is a narrow, hidden path surrounded by pits and traps—a divine obstacle course. One false move and we plunge to disaster. One mistake and God's anger awaits. No wonder Carolyn was nervous about making the wrong choice.

I had this same fear when I was entering college and deciding what I should do with my life. I went to my father and asked, "Should I be an actor, a writer, a counselor, or a teacher?"

He answered, "I'm not concerned about what you do. I care about who you become."

I didn't like his answer back then, but I have grown to appreciate its wisdom. I think our Father in heaven shares this attitude. God is less concerned about the specifics of our lives and more interested in the kind of people we become.

I refused to tell Carolyn what to do. I believe part of becoming a mature person is learning to make good choices. We did talk about her options, and I assured her God would not punish her for working on Sunday. Jesus thought there are vastly more important issues than whether or not we are sitting in a pew on Sunday morning. I asked her, regardless of which job she chose, how she hoped to establish God's kingdom. She stared back at me blankly.

In fairness to Carolyn, it was a difficult question and one many of us fail to consider. We seldom notice that Jesus taught his disciples to seek God's kingdom and will before making their petitions and requests. "Thy kingdom come and thy will be done" precedes "Give us this day our daily bread." Jesus told his disciples to focus on God's will rather than on their needs. He said, "Seek first his kingdom and his righteousness, and all these things (i.e., material needs) will be given to you as well" (Matt. 6:33).

Even more revealing, Jesus told his disciples to focus on God's kingdom before they focused on God's will. Understanding God's kingdom is the key to discerning God's will. To seek God's will without understanding his kingdom is like setting out on a journey without a map. Once we glimpse the kingdom of God, finding our path becomes simpler. The question becomes "How can I work to establish the kingdom of God?"

Unfortunately, most of us are like Carolyn. We pray "thy will be done" with little thought about "thy kingdom come." We seek God's will in our corner of the earth with little regard for establishing his kingdom to the four corners of the earth. When we seek God's will for ourselves alone, we seek a means of blessing rather than guidance in advancing God's kingdom in the world.

Many of us have ignored our responsibility to be about the work of the kingdom. We have assumed God's kingdom will only come when Christ returns. This is not what Jesus taught. Jesus began his ministry by preaching, "Repent, for the kingdom of God is near" (Matt. 4:17). Since we are still waiting for the apocalypse, Jesus must have meant something other than the end of the world.

We are not the first to be confused about the timing of God's kingdom. Jesus was asked when the kingdom of God would come. He replied, "The kingdom of God does not come with your careful observation, nor will people say, 'Here it is,' or 'There it is,' because the kingdom of God is within you" (Luke 17:20–21).

This is marvelously clear. The kingdom of God is not

something external that we await. It is within us
be born on earth as it is in heaven. When we pray
dom come," we are not making a request. We'r
vow. We are pledging our willingness to allow G   ...ng-
dom to be established in and through us.

Thy Kingdom Come

Jesus said, "My kingdom is not of this world" (John 18:36).
He was reminding us that the kingdoms of this world are
not the kingdom of God. There are many competing kingdoms in this world: dictatorships and democracies, socialism
and capitalism, corporations and religions. Some have been
more successful than others.

Often Christianity, rather than standing in critique
and opposition to these kingdoms, has imitated them. We
are easily seduced by power, glamour, and success. When
Constantine offered the church political power and legitimacy, it traded the kingdom of God for an earthly throne.
The popes eventually led armies, as the church became the
"Holy Roman Empire." When Luther rebelled against such
abuses, his reformation was largely successful because
German princes wanted to be free of clergy domination.

In England, Henry VIII made himself the leader of the
church in order to justify his many marriages. The Church of

England was his political lackey. The Puritans were persecuted by his church and came to America to establish the kingdom of God. Of course, their kingdom was one where those who did not believe as they did were persecuted and killed. They used their power to do to others exactly what had been done to them.

It is easy to see compromises of ages past. It is much more difficult to recognize how easily we are seduced today. When I was in seminary, there was a move to redefine the pastor as a CEO, the church as a business, and parishioners as customers. In many ways, this movement fueled the emergence of megachurches. These churches, designed to address every imaginable need of middle-class Americans, have as many as thirty thousand members and budgets in the millions. One megachurch pastor bragged, "We have beat the world at its own game."

This desire "to beat the world at its own game" explains how prosperity theology has gained dominance in many religious circles. It has twisted the gospel into a vehicle for personal profit, another strategy of self-enhancement in a cultural marketplace of greed. Promoted most heavily on "Christian" television, the good news of Jesus becomes akin to a good stock tip or picking the right horse. The righteous get rich, and poor have only their sinfulness to blame. The dirty secret of this kingdom is that most of the wealth ends up in the hands of those promoting this theology.

In the midst of so many competing secular and religious kingdoms, it might seem impossible to discern what the kingdom of God should look like. But it isn't. In fact, Jesus spent most of his time describing the kingdom of God. His descriptions and analogies make it obvious the kingdom of God is unlike the kingdoms of this world.

Donald Kraybill, in his book *The Upside-Down Kingdom,* suggests "the kingdom of God points to an inverted, or upside-down, way of life that contrasts with the prevailing social order."[1] In this upside-down kingdom, the first shall be last and the last shall be first, the exalted will be humbled and the humbled will be exalted, sinners are forgiven and welcomed while the self-righteous are chastised, the poor are blessed and the rich are condemned, the lost are found and the dead are made alive, the lion lays down with the lamb and spears are beaten into pruning hooks. This is the language of the kingdom of God.

Indeed, the consistency with which the kingdom of God is the opposite of the kingdoms of this world should serve as a warning. Conventional wisdom and common sense are not signs of the kingdom of God. Jesus warned, "I tell you the truth, the tax collectors and the prostitutes are entering the kingdom of God ahead of you" (Matt. 21:31). He announced, "Blessed are you who are poor, for yours is the kingdom of God" (Luke 6:20). He shocked his disciples by saying, "It is easier for a camel to go through the eye of a needle that for a rich man to enter the kingdom of God" (Matt. 19:24). His descriptions of the kingdom of God challenge human measures of success.

Jesus began many of his stories with the words "The kingdom of God is like . . ." He compared the kingdom of God to a seed, yeast, a hidden treasure, and a pearl of great price. It is small and easy to miss, yet endowed with great power and worth. The kingdom of God is usually the very opposite of what we would expect. It is a kingdom founded on grace rather than works, grounded in love rather than legalism, and open to all rather than to a few. Most important, it is a kingdom most concerned about those who have been ignored, neglected, and even oppressed by the kingdoms of this world.

Mary, the mother of Jesus, anticipated the kingdom her son would proclaim. She said, "God has scattered those who are proud in their inmost thoughts. He has brought down rulers from their thrones, but has lifted up the humble. He has filled the hungry with good things, but has sent the rich away empty" (Luke 1:51–53).

Jesus began his ministry with similar words: "The Spirit of the Lord is on me, because he has anointed me to preach good news to the poor. He has sent me to proclaim freedom for the prisoners and recovery of sight for the blind, to release the oppressed, to proclaim the year of the Lord's favor" (Luke 4:18–19).

Unfortunately, the kingdom Mary and Jesus envisioned and celebrated has yet to come. If this is the will of God, why has this not occurred? Jesus must have anticipated this complaint. He told an intriguing story to those "who thought the kingdom of God was going to appear at once" (Luke 19:11). He spoke of a king who was preparing for a long journey and left his affairs in the hands of three servants. When he returned, he sent for these servants so they could account for themselves. The first two had taken what he had given and multiplied it. The last servant hid his blessing away. The king was less than pleased (Matt. 25:14–30).

I wonder how often we are like the last servant. We sit and await Christ's return and do little to advance the kingdom of God. Jesus seemed to think the kingdom of God would only appear as we work to eliminate poverty, free those who are prisoners (either of their own making or of others), give sight to the blind (especially those blind to their responsibility), and release the oppressed. Perhaps one of the reasons the kingdom of God has yet to appear is because millions of Christians have prayed the Prayer of Jesus without keeping its vows.

"Thy kingdom come and thy will be done" has been wishful thinking rather than a call to action. Being a

Christian has been a status rather than a calling. Once, after Jesus had spoken, a woman said, "Blessed is the mother who gave you birth and nursed you." Jesus replied, "Blessed rather are those who hear the word of God and obey it" (Luke 11:27–28). Too often, we relax in our good fortune in being born and nurtured in the church. We consider ourselves blessed. Jesus called us to take seriously our responsibility to establish the kingdom of God. We are to do the will of the Father.

Thy Will Be Done

What is the will of God? We often make this a selfish search. What does God want for me? What is the best path for me? However, in the context of kingdom of God, seeking God's will is always discerning our role in making earth as it is in heaven.

John of Patmos proclaimed this vision. He said, "Now the dwelling of God is with men, and he will live with them. They will be his people, and God himself will be with them and be their God. He will wipe every tear from their eyes. There will be no more death or mourning or crying or pain, for the old order of things has passed away" (Rev. 21:3–4). Unfortunately, most Christians are not committed to making this a reality.

Many Christians are obsessed with Christ's return. They ignore his warning that "no one will know the hour or the day." Within my lifetime, many have announced Christ's imminent arrival. This fascination with God's ultimate intervention in the world has become an excuse for inactivity. Often I hear Christians talk about some terrible problem in our culture or some deep need in our world and end their discussion with the words, "Well, it won't be solved until Christ returns." Jesus must weep whenever he hears those words. I can almost hear him saying, "You are my body. You are my hands and my feet and my mouth. The kingdom of God is within you. Let it out!"

One day, Jesus came to the pool at Bethesda. The small pool was surrounded with the blind, lame, and paralyzed. They lay waiting for the waters of the pool to be stirred. Superstition said that when the waters were stirred, the first one to be immersed in the pool would be healed.

Jesus came to the pool and saw a man who had been disabled for thirty-eight years. He asked him, "Do you want to get well?" The man replied, "I have no one to help me into the pool when the water is stirred. While I am trying to get in, someone else goes down before me." Then Jesus said, "Get up! Pick up your mat and walk!" (John 5:6–8).

So many of us today are like that invalid lying by the pool. We are crippled, blind, and paralyzed. We are waiting for something magical to happen. We are frustrated and discouraged when nothing seems to change. We want God's kingdom to come and his will to be done, but our only action is to complain.

Do we really want God's kingdom to come and God's will to be done? Or are we satisfied with the status quo? Are we willing to make our prayers preparation for action? Or will our prayers become a substitute for doing the will of God? Do we only want God's kingdom to come and his will to be done if it requires nothing of us?

We make excuses. "Of course we want your kingdom to come, Lord. We've been praying the Lord's Prayer since childhood, but your kingdom has still not come." We take the prayer he taught us to pray and make it our alibi. I think I know what Jesus would answer. He would say, "Get up. Pick up your mat and walk! Bring my kingdom to this world."

Some do stand and walk.

Lucius Newsom is one such man. A retired Baptist preacher, he felt called to feed the hungry and clothe the naked. He decided Jesus was serious when he said, "When you do it for the least of these, then you do it for me." So this elderly man, retired and on a fixed income, began to fill his van with food and clothes and share the little he had with people in need.

A friend of mine is a pastor, and his church heard about Lucius. They decided they would give him money to help him buy food and clothes. The head of the mission committee took a check to Lucius one Saturday. He arrived to find Lucius setting up tables in a vacant lot and placing food and clothes out for people to take, and surrounded by people patiently waiting to receive his help. He walked up to Lucius and handed him the check.

Lucius wouldn't accept it. He said, "I don't need your money. I need your hands. But if you want to stay here and help me serve these people, I'd be obliged." That is the language of the kingdom. Lucius only accepted the financial gift after several months of observing the hearts of those volunteers. Were they really interested in establishing the kingdom? Or were they acting out of guilt or pride?

Establishing the kingdom of God is not about large financial donations, ministries that look more like corporations, or churches that resemble malls. It will not come with careful observation and with cries of "Here it is" or "There it is." It will appear in the most unexpected places. It will seem small and insignificant in contrast to the kingdoms of this world. It will be most obvious in those places where men and women are acting in ways counter to the kingdoms of this world.

The workers of the kingdom of God will be recognizable because they always seem odd. They do the will of God even when it seems absurd. John the Baptist wore camel's hair and preached repentance in the desert. He would be locked up in a mental institution today. St. Francis of Assisi thought caring for insects, birds, and animals was important to God. He would be ridiculed as a New Age tree hugger. Adoniram Judson spent six years in Burma before he had his first convert. He would be pulled from the mission field as a failure. Sojourner Truth was unwilling to allow the color of her skin or her gender to keep her from preaching. She would be scorned as a feminist. Mother Teresa considered dying Hindus and Buddhists worth her kindest attention. She is still a puzzle to so many.

These people were living in a kingdom where the world is upside down. Doing the will of God was not about praying in the morning and expecting results that afternoon. It was a conviction that God is slowly and carefully overcoming the kingdoms of this world and establishing his kingdom. They saw heaven on earth even while they worked in the hellholes of the world. They were willing to play a small part in that cosmic drama.

Unfortunately, when it comes to the kingdom of God, "the harvest is plentiful, but the workers are few" (Matt. 9:37). Whenever I read a poll announcing that 90 percent of all Americans consider themselves Christians, I wonder. When I hear that there are two billion Christians in this world, I wonder. What would it mean if every Christian in the world prayed "Thy kingdom come and thy will be done" as a vow? What would it mean if the Prayer of Jesus became a prayer of commitment? I wonder.

The Prayer of Commitment

Prayer is uniting our will with the will of God. It is not an attempt to get God to do our will. It is desiring to do what delights God. It is discovering that what pleases God will ultimately bring us joy as well. It is following in his footsteps even when he leads where we fear to go.

One of the more powerful stories in the Bible is the one of Jesus praying in the Garden of Gethsemane. He knows one of his own disciples has already betrayed him. He knows the forces in Jerusalem that oppose him are preparing to arrest him. He knows they will not be satisfied until he is dead. So he finds a quiet place and prays.

His words are so human. "My soul is overwhelmed with sorrow to the point of death. Daddy (Abba), everything is possible for you. Take this cup from me" (Mark 14:36). I know that prayer. I prayed it when my mother was dying of cancer. I prayed it when my marriage was on the rocks. I prayed it when my daughter developed a tumor. I suspect we've all had cups we've asked God to take from us.

But Jesus doesn't end his prayer with his desire. He ends with these words of faith, "Yet not what I will, but what you will." He was praying the very prayer he had taught his disciples to pray. "Thy kingdom come. Thy will be done, on earth as it is in heaven." The deepest desire of his heart was for the will of God to be his will. He wanted to do those things that would establish the kingdom of God, even if his obedience led to a cross.

I want to be very careful at this point. I do not mean to imply it was God's will that Jesus die on a cross. God's desire was for people to welcome Jesus as a herald of God's kingdom. God wanted men and women to embrace this kingdom and live a new way. The will of God has always been to see his kingdom established on earth as it is in heaven.

Unfortunately, we have always resisted this call. We have a long history of killing those who seek to proclaim and establish the kingdom of God. Jesus, shortly before we killed him, pointed out, "You say, 'If we had lived in the days of our forefathers, we would not have taken part with them in shedding the blood of the prophets.' So you testify against yourselves that you are the descendants of those who murdered the prophets" (Matt. 23:30–31).

The cross was not God's will. It was additional evidence of our resistance to both God's kingdom and will. The cross is a vivid example of the power, violence, and death typical of the kingdoms of this world. The resurrection is God's proclamation that the kingdoms of this world will not have the final word.

Jesus said, "I tell you the truth, unless a kernel of wheat falls to the ground and dies, it remains only a single seed. But if it dies, it produces many seeds" (John 12:24). Jesus was talking about himself and about us. Although I do not believe Jesus sought death, he was so committed to God's kingdom he was willing to die. Praying "Thy kingdom come and thy will be done" is a prayer of total commitment.

This level of self-denial is something all of us resist. Only a confidence in the love of our Father in heaven makes such sacrifice possible. At Gethsemane, Jesus demonstrated his willingness to die in order to see God's kingdom advanced. He also proclaimed his trust in God.

Trusting God is the bedrock of prayer. We are trusting that God knows the whole even when we see dimly. We are believing "that in all things God works for good for those who love him and have been called according to his purpose" (Rom. 8:28). We are accepting God's will as preferable to our will. Even when we experience struggle rather than victory and suffering rather than ease, we are convinced our Father in heaven can be trusted.

Brennan Manning says:

Uncompromising trust in the love of God inspires us to thank God for the spiritual darkness that envelops us, for the loss of income, for the nagging arthritis that is so painful, and to pray from the heart, "Abba, into your hands I entrust my body, mind and spirit and this entire day—morning, after-noon, evening and night. Whatever you want of me, I want of me, falling into you and trusting in you in the midst of life. Into your heart I entrust my heart, feeble, distracted, insecure, uncertain. Abba, unto you I abandon myself in Jesus our Lord. Amen." [2]

This is a prayer reminiscent of what Jesus prayed at Gethsemane and of "Thy kingdom come and thy will be done." Only such radical trust makes self-denial and extravagant generosity possible. Such prayers seek strength in the midst of tribulation rather than comfort and ease. They recognize that if establishing the kingdom of God cost Jesus his life, we can expect it to cost us as well.

Some, especially the most comfortable, complain of the harshness of such prayers. When our lives are centered around a pursuit of happiness, these prayers seem ridiculous. Only when we become committed to God's kingdom can such prayers become a source of joy. Only then does Paul's confession make sense. "I want to know Christ and the power of his resurrection and the fellowship of sharing in his sufferings, becoming like him in his death" (Phil. 3:10).

Bonhoeffer said, "When God calls a man, he bids him come and die."[3] This is not the usual evangelical invitation. Most churches downplay the responsibilities of a relationship with God and emphasize the benefits. We are afraid people will not accept such a high calling. Our reluctance to proclaim the kingdom of God robs Christianity of its purpose for being. No wonder many have rejected the church. If the church is not committed to changing the world, it becomes irrelevant.

The kingdoms of this world are not afraid to demand total commitment. When the Japanese bombed Pearl Harbor, President Franklin D. Roosevelt did not hesitate to call on every man and woman to work and sacrifice. We memorialize those who have fallen in battle and call this the "supreme sacrifice."

The supreme sacrifice is not to die for your country. It is when we are willing to commit ourselves completely to the kingdom of God. Jesus said, "My command is this: Love each other as I have loved you. Greater love has no one than this, that he lay down his life for his friends" (John 15:12–13). Establishing the kingdom of God will require no less sacrifice than the kingdoms of this world demand.

What would it mean if Christians totally committed themselves to the kingdom of God? For most of us, it would not require our deaths. However, it would demand our self-denial. We would have to be willing to lay down our lives—our kingdoms, wills, and agendas—and give ourselves generously to our brothers and sisters.

"Thy kingdom come. Thy will be done, on earth as it is in heaven" would need to become our vow. We would need to stop pretending the will of God is a mystery. Jesus made God's concerns clear. God wants us to feed the hungry, give water to the thirsty, clothe the naked, care for the sick, and visit the prisoners. God wants us committed to seeing that all of God's children receive their daily bread.

1. Donald Kraybill, *The Upside-Down Kingdom* (Herald Press, 1978), p. 19. This has been one of the most influential books in my life. His discussions of the contrasts between the kingdom of God and the kingdoms of this world are startling.

2. Brennan Manning, *Ruthless Trust* (HarperSanFrancisco, 2000), p. 11. Anchored in his own struggles, this discussion of trust makes any attempt to manipulate God seem even more shameful.

3. Dietrich Bonhoeffer, *The Cost of Discipleship* (SCM Press, 1959), p. 7.

~ ~

Give Us

Give us this day our daily bread.

When they had finished eating, Jesus said to Simon Peter,
  "Simon son of John, do you truly love me more than these?"
"Yes, Lord," he said, "you know that I love you."
Jesus said, "Feed my lambs."
Again Jesus said, "Simon son of John, do you truly love me?"
He answered, "Yes, Lord, you know that I love you."
Jesus said, "Take care of my sheep."
The third time he said to him, "Simon son of John, do you
  love me?"
Peter was hurt because Jesus asked him a third time, "Do you
  love me?" He said, "Lord, you know all things; you know
  that I love you."
Jesus said, "Feed my sheep." (John 21:15–17)

In this encounter, Jesus connected love and meeting the basic needs of people. He thought compassion such a priority he asked Peter to affirm his commitment three times. I wonder how this conversation would sound if Jesus were to ask me his question.

When we had finished eating, Jesus said to me, "Jim, do you truly love me more than these?

"Yes, Lord," I said, "you know that I love you. I preach so eloquently that old women weep, old men growl 'Amen,' young women see visions, and young men dream dreams. I articulate the truths of the faith in such a manner that the greatest intellectual is challenged and the greatest dullard is enlightened. I fill pews, and people ask for copies of my sermons."

Jesus said, "Feed my lambs."

Again Jesus said, "Jim, do you truly love me?

I answered, "Yes, Lord, you know that I love you. I grew up in the church. I attended a Christian college. I went to seminary for four years. I've studied the Bible and systematized my theology. When it comes to love, I can explain the difference between eros, philia, *and* agape. *I've even memorized the thirteenth chapter of First Corinthians."*

Jesus said, "Take care of my sheep."

The third time he said to me, "Jim, do you love me?"

I was hurt because Jesus asked me a third time, "Do you love me?" I said, "Lord, you know all things; you know I that I love you. I've developed programs serving senior citizens, empty-nesters, the parents of teenagers, teenagers, young adults, young marrieds, singles, children, and infants. I've doubled the worship attendance and balanced the budget. I could teach a workshop on church growth."

Jesus said, "Feed my sheep."

I worry that we in the church are not hearing what Jesus said. Pastors and churches expend 99 percent of their time and energy on eloquent preaching, theological indoctrination, and institutional maintenance. Our priorities are not the priorities of Jesus. He wanted to make certain Peter would feed and care for the sheep. He asked him to give them something to eat.

The Priorities of the Kingdom

I used to believe preaching, teaching, and organizing were the priorities of the church. I spiritualized the command to "feed the sheep." In a culture of affluence, it is so tempting to interpret feeding the sheep as taking care of us. Feeding becomes worship and Sunday school. Organizing becomes keeping the sheep comfortable and in the fold. Only when I began to pastor an inner-city church did I realize how difficult it is to preach, teach, and organize people whose basic needs aren't being met.

When we spiritualize the commands of the gospel, we fail to acknowledge the deep poverty of the people to whom Jesus preached and taught. We ignore his consistent emphasis on meeting the physical needs of the oppressed. We relegate the cry of the needy to the back of the line and the bottom of the budget. We make the church into a social club and a religious discussion group.

Jesus taught his disciples to pray "Give us this day our daily bread" because finding enough to eat was a serious problem. Jesus was making clear the first priority in establishing the kingdom of God—basic human needs must be met. When the church fails to feed God's children, the church fails. When an American church with the resources to feed the world squanders this blessing selfishly, the American church sins. We betray the kingdom of God.

In Matthew 25, Jesus described the acts of those "blessed by my Father" and inheritors of the kingdom. He said, "I was hungry and you gave me something to eat, I was thirsty and you gave me something to drink, I was a stranger and you invited me in, I needed clothes and you clothed me, I was sick and you looked after me, I was in prison and you came to visit me" (vv. 35–36). When those he was addressing asked when they had done these things, he replied, "Whatever you did for one of the least of these brothers of mine, you did for me" (v. 40).

The priorities of the kingdom of God couldn't be clearer. We are to feed the hungry, provide clean water for the thirsty, open our homes to the homeless, clothe the naked, care for the sick, and visit those in prison. These should be the priorities of the church. James, addressing the early church, said, "Religion that God our Father accepts as pure and faultless is this: to look after orphans and widows in their distress and to keep oneself from being polluted by the world" (James 1:27).

At the college I attended, the pollution of the world was defined as dancing, drinking, and smoking. Drinking and smoking polluted the body, and the body was God's temple. Dancing was prohibited because it always led to sexual immorality—the ultimate act of pollution. Every student had to sign a "lifestyle statement" that pledged abstinence from dancing (and thereby sexual sin), drinking, and smoking. We signed nothing forbidding greed.

Greed is the unchallenged sin in the American church. Orphans and widows go without because religion and greed walk hand in hand. In our infatuation with material gain, we have made greed into a virtue. Success in our culture, and often in the church, is measured in dollars. It's no mystery why many find prosperity theology so attractive. It justifies our culture's values. We interpret our excess as a sign of God's blessing and favor rather than evidence of our avarice. We not only insist on having more than we need; we defend our gluttony as divinely ordained.

We ignore or spiritualize Jesus' command to feed his sheep. We become the shepherds Ezekiel warned of. "You eat the curds, clothe yourselves with the wool and slaughter the choice animals, but you do not take care of the flock. You have not strengthened the weak or healed the sick or bound up the injured" (Ezek. 34:3–4). We have cared for ourselves and let the rest of the world be damned.

God's response to greed is as clear as his priorities. "I myself will judge between the fat sheep and the lean sheep, because you shove with flank and shoulder, butting all the weak sheep with your horns until you have driven them away. I will save the flock and they will no longer be plundered" (Ezek. 34:20–22). I seldom hear these passages preached in the American church. They so obviously indict us. We are the fat sheep. The inequalities of the world are the result of our greed.

Greed not only does great damage to the poor; it is also our spiritual affliction. It is a sign of faithlessness. We hoard more than we need today because we are afraid God will not provide for tomorrow. We are like the Israelites who, though God had promised to supply daily manna in the wilderness, insisted on collecting more than they needed. We call this prudence, but for the children of God it is really distrust.

We are like the rich fool. Jesus said, "The ground of a certain man produced a good crop. He thought to himself, 'What shall I do? I have no place to store my crops'" (Luke 12:16–17). He decided to build bigger barns. He was unwilling to trust that the God who had supplied his needs today would also supply them tomorrow. It didn't occur to him to seek those who were hungry and feed them. He didn't even consider the priorities of God.

He sounds remarkably like us. When we have excess, we don't even ask, "What shall we do?" The answer is so ingrained. We store it away. We invest in mutual funds. We establish endowments. We build bigger houses and more opulent sanctuaries. We seldom do what a church in Texas did. After sending mission teams to Mexico to build housing, they decided to take the building fund for their new sanctuary and use it to build dozens of more homes. Far more often we rationalize our greed and selfishness. We fail to understand the proper use of prosperity.

The Proper Use of Prosperity

If we were to shrink the world's population to 100 people, with all the ratios remaining the same, there would be 59

Asians, 15 Europeans, 9 South and Central Americans, 11 Africans, and 6 citizens of the United States and Canada. There would be 52 females and 48 males. Thirty people would be white and 70 would be of other races. Thirty would be Christian and 70 would be of other religions. Thirty would be able to read and 70 would not.

Although we in the United States are only a small percentage of the world's population, we possess 59 percent of the world's wealth. If we have food in the refrigerator, clothes on our back, and a roof over our heads, then we are already richer than 75 percent of the world. Hot water, indoor plumbing, cars, televisions, telephones, and computers are extravagant luxuries in a world where five hundred million people are starving to death.[1] What does it mean to pray "Give us this day our daily bread" when we are so blessed?

A few years ago I had the opportunity to travel to Honduras, the second-poorest country in our hemisphere, as part of a mission team. We worked with the inhabitants of a mountain village to build a water system. It was a jarring experience, as we saw firsthand the terrible inequalities of the world. I remember the moment I became aware of my wealth.

Our group had taken several large plastic jars of peanut butter on our trip. When our stomachs began to reject the local food, some of us lived on peanut butter and crackers.

One day we finished a jar and threw it away. A few minutes later we heard two women arguing loudly. They had found the jar and were fighting over it. They wanted to use it to store rice or beans. What does it mean to pray "Give us this day our daily bread" when some are fighting over our trash?

When we arrived home from our trip to Honduras, we were asked to share what we had learned. Person after person stood and said things such as, "I never realized how blessed we are in America," "I am so thankful I was born in the United States," and "I will never take my blessings for granted again." I was glad to hear these words, but I am always saddened when we count our blessings without remembering our responsibility.

It is crucial to remember than none of us did anything to deserve most of the blessings we experience. Simply being born in the United States is an enormous advantage. When I take into account the country of my birth, my loving parents, my excellent education, and my good health, then I become one of a very small group—those who have been blessed beyond measure. Of course, the question for American Christians is whether we are blessed as a sign of God's favor or blessed in order to be a blessing.

Recently I was listening to a Christian radio program on which someone asked about the unfairness of some being born in a country like India or China, where they wouldn't hear about Jesus. The host of the show suggested that since God knows everything, God would allow only those who would reject him to be born in such places. That is ugly theology. It implies that those born in predominantly Christian nations were God's favorites before they were born. It also suggests the death of children in India, China, and Africa is less tragic since they are destined for hell anyway.

Let me suggest a far more obvious reason we are blessed. We have been given abundance as a responsibility. Jesus said, "From everyone who has been given much, much will be demanded; and from the one who has been entrusted with much, much more will be asked" (Luke 12:48). Our blessing has a purpose. God intends for us to care for our brothers and sisters. His blessing is our resource for establishing the kingdom of God. When those of us who are materially blessed pray, "Give us this day our daily bread," we are accepting our responsibility to feed the hungry of the world.

The proper response to prosperity is not indulgence. Nor is it the seeking of even more blessing. Prosperity and blessing are not ends in themselves. We are not to eat, drink, and be merry. We are not to feast while the world famishes. We are not to celebrate our good fortune as we pity those less blessed.

The proper response to prosperity is not justification. We are not to pretend we deserve what we possess. We are not to argue that our blessing is a reward for our goodness or hard work. We are not to imply starving children have only themselves to blame.

The proper response to prosperity is not guilt. We are not to bemoan the unfairness of the world. We are not to demand to know why those richer than us don't give more. We are not to make our donations and then wash our hands.

The proper response to prosperity, even modest prosperity, is compassion.

One day, Jesus and his disciples were seeking a quiet place to eat and rest. They set off in a boat, but the crowd followed them. Jesus, seeing their great need, had compassion for them. He taught them, he healed them, and he loved them. The disciples were not quite as compassionate. They had been looking forward to a quiet little supper with Jesus and instead they had hardly even had a chance to speak to him. He had been surrounded by people all day. Now it was growing dark and the disciples were becoming frustrated.

One of them came to Jesus and said, "This is a remote place and it's already very late. Send the people away so they can go into the surrounding countryside and villages and buy themselves something to eat."

Jesus responded, "You give them something to eat."

The Bible tells us one of them said, "That would take eight months of a man's wage! Are we to go and spend that much on bread and give it to them to eat?" (Mark 6:35–37).

I expect that wasn't their only objection. I imagine they listed the same excuses we give today for not being compassionate.

I can hear John saying, "Jesus, you are such a soft touch. These people made bad choices. They should have realized they would need food when they came out here. Do you want us to reward that irresponsibility?"

I can imagine Matthew saying, "Lord, you are so naïve. I know these people. They're the ones who never pay their taxes. They're lazy and always looking for a handout. Do you want us to encourage that behavior?"

I can picture Judas holding up the common purse and saying, "Master, we need be good stewards of what we've been given. If we feed these people today, then they'll just be hungry tomorrow. Do you want us to throw money down a rat's hole?"

There are always excuses for not being compassionate.

Jesus simply asked, "How many loaves do you have?" Then he took those five loaves and two fish, gave thanks for them, and told the disciples to share them with the people. You know the rest of the story: everyone ate and there were twelve baskets of broken pieces of bread and fish left over.

It was a miracle, but I don't think it was supernatural. I think what happened is that those people saw Jesus take the little food he had and offer it to them. I believe they were deeply moved by his compassion and generosity. Suddenly, the baskets and packages of food that had been hoarded and hidden by thousands of people were freely offered to those around them.

You may think that isn't much of a miracle, but it's always miraculous when people turn from selfishness and decide to be gracious. It was two thousand years ago, and it would be today. What would it mean if the church took seriously the call of Jesus to give the hungry of the world something to eat? What would it mean if Christians and churches took the money we have hidden in bank accounts and guarded by mutual funds and offered it to the hungry of the world? In 1998, it was determined that it would take only thirteen billion dollars to eliminate starvation in the world. In 1999, the American church spent six billion dollars just on new buildings. How would the rest of the world react if they saw churches committing themselves to feeding the world instead of building luxurious sanctuaries, gyms, and family-life centers?

I was reading the other day about the early church. Historians now believe the primary reason the early church grew was not because of an aggressive evangelism program, not because of an expensive building project, and not because of a worldwide media campaign. They believe Christianity spread so quickly because Christians took seriously Jesus' command to be compassionate.[2] In the Roman world, where 5 percent of the people were wealthy and the rest were either poor or slaves, the willingness of Christians to feed the hungry, clothe the naked, care for the sick, and visit those in prison was miraculous.

Unfortunately, the compassion of Christians is no longer legendary. I was watching a television program in which a Christian from Sudan was being interviewed. He asked, "How can our rich Christian brothers and sisters in America ignore the fact that we in Sudan are starving to death?" I thought to myself, "I'm glad I don't have to answer that question!" And then the Holy Spirit tapped me on the shoulder and said, "You do."

What would you say to that man? I think I would have to apologize. I wouldn't want to admit how many times my prayer has really been "Give me this day my daily luxuries." I wouldn't want to confess to how seldom I have even thought about his plight. I wouldn't want to have to tell him that American Christians give only about 3 percent of their income to their churches and charities. I certainly wouldn't want to mention how much food we throw away after a church dinner.

That man in Sudan and I both pray, "Give us this day our daily bread." For him, it is a cry of desperation. For me, it needs to become a vow of generosity. When I say those words, I am not asking for bread for myself. I'm twenty pounds overweight. I could use a little less daily bread. When I pray "Give us this day our daily bread," I am pledging to do all in my power to see that my brother in Sudan has daily bread.

"Give us this day our daily bread" is a prayer of equality. It is a recognition of God's interest in more than just my needs. God cares for the needs of all. What God desires is not for some to be prosperous and others to be impoverished. God desires equality. He wants everyone to have enough.

The Prayer of Equality

I am intrigued when churches claim to be "apostolic." This usually means they think they are like the early church and other churches are not. Being "apostolic" is defined as speaking in tongues, adhering to some strict doctrine, or being in direct succession to the apostle Peter. I never hear anyone suggesting that we should adopt the early church's attitude toward human need.

The Bible does say the early church preached, taught, broke bread together, and exhibited wonders and miraculous signs. It also says, "There were no needy persons among them. For from time to time those who owned lands or houses sold them, brought the money from the sales and put it at the apostles' feet, and it was distributed to anyone who had need" (Acts 4:34–35). I yearn for a church committed to having "no needy persons among them."

Of course, this can happen only if some of us are willing to sell lands or houses. One of the most difficult ideas for those of us in prosperous countries to accept is that our prosperity is built on the backs of the poor. The reason I have so much more than I need is because someone else has so much less than they need. On my trip to Honduras I discovered why I can buy bananas for twenty-five cents a pound. All that is required is that banana pickers in Honduras be paid twenty-five cents a day.

Our favorite justification for inequality is the adage, "Anyone who works hard enough can succeed." We in the United States want to believe that everyone in the whole world could be like us if they would work a little harder. This simply isn't true. Everyone in the world cannot have as many cars (one for every two persons) as those of us in the United States. If they did, the oil reserves would disappear overnight.

The problem in Honduras is not laziness. The people there simply lack the resources we have hoarded for ourselves. We have cut the pie in unequal pieces and then act surprised when so many go away hungry. I know how my father handled situations in which I was unfair to my younger brothers. He took their side.

Robert McAfee Brown says, "The source of hope for third world Christians is that God takes sides in the struggle and that God takes their side." He explains that a God who sided with tyrants would be evil and a God who sided with no one would be indifferent. "Only a God siding with the oppressed would be a God of justice."[3] The solution to world hunger is not forcing the poor to work harder; it is for the rich to work for equality.

I grow discouraged when we defend our prosperity as a result of God's special favor or of our hard work. I am dismayed when poverty is casually dismissed as the result of laziness or sin. I am bewildered by our ability to pray "Give us this day our daily bread" without hearing it as a call to generosity. To pray "Give us" must be a commitment to meeting the basic needs of every person in the world. When we say "us," it must mean all of us.

The first priority in establishing the kingdom of God is feeding the sheep. It is not enough for us to respond when there is a terrible hurricane, famine, or epidemic. The daily misery of millions should deeply trouble me. Often I blissfully forget their struggle and my ease. I wonder why. Is it because I think the problems are too big? Is it because the crisis is too far away? Or is it because I am afraid of what it would require of me to address the inequalities in this world?

It will require resolve. In order to feed the world, I will need to abandon my desire for more, especially when I already have enough. I will need to commit myself to finding effective ways to transfer my resources to needy places. I will need to demand that my church make world hunger a higher priority than new carpeting. I will need to lobby my representatives in Congress to use more of our money to buy food and less to buy weapons.

It will require sacrifice. In order to feed the world, I may need to eat a little less. I may have to give up some of my luxuries. I may need to alter my lifestyle. I will need to deny myself in order to give to others. Self-denial is something I always resist.

Paul struggled with this same resistance two thousand years ago. He wrote the wealthy church in Corinth about the poverty of the church in Jerusalem. He asked them to be generous. Apparently they were less than enthused by his request. In response to their complaints, Paul said, "Our desire is not that others might be relieved while you are hard pressed, but that there might be equality" (2 Cor. 8:13). Equality! What a wonderful concept.

Wouldn't it be wonderful if everyone had enough to eat? Wouldn't it be wonderful if everyone had clean water to drink? Wouldn't it be wonderful if everyone had a roof over their head? Wouldn't it be wonderful if everyone had adequate health care? Wouldn't it be wonderful if Christians realized this doesn't require God's supernatural intervention? It only requires a miracle. It requires you and me to take seriously the words, "Give us this day our daily bread." Until we eliminate poverty, everything else we do is a mockery of God's will.

We must understand what Jesus was teaching Peter when he asked him three times, "Do you love me?" We cannot proclaim the love of God if we refuse to feed his lambs. Our theological orthodoxy is meaningless if we don't take care of his sheep. The buildings and budgets of our religious institutions are an abomination if we don't feed his sheep. We cannot pray "Forgive us our sins" with sincerity if we continue to allow children to starve to death. There is no sin greater than allowing some of our brothers or sisters to die when we have the capacity to save them.

1. The statistics used in this chapter are largely based on the 1998 U.N. Human Development Report. I often wonder if the United Nations has such a bad reputation in some Christian circles because it challenges our complacency.

2. *The Evangelization of the Roman Empire* by Glenn Hinson (Mercer University Press, 1981) and *The Rise of Christianity: A Sociologist Reconsiders History* by Rodney Stark (Princeton University Press, 1996) are two of the more recent books making this argument.

3. Robert McAfee Brown, *Unexpected News: Reading the Bible with Third World Eyes* (Westminster Press, 1984), p. 41. This is a wonderful examination of how the poor read the Bible. He challenges the way rich Christians reinterpret stories that are plainly directed at us.

~ ~

FIVE

Forgive Us

Forgive us our sins, as we forgive those who sin against us.

When our two children were young, we took them to an amusement park. Our finances were tight. We had saved for several months for the trip. It was supposed to be a great day—a time of fun and relaxation for our family.

We were barely out of the driveway when my daughter and son began to fight in the backseat of the car. It was a big backseat. Three adults could sit in that backseat comfortably. This made it even more mystifying when my daughter kept yelling, "He's touching me," and my son kept replying, "Well, she's touching me."

This went on mile after mile. Finally, in a relatively calm voice, I announced, "If I hear about anyone touching anyone else, I'm going to turn this car around and go home." It was an idle threat. I knew it. They knew it. But they did quit fighting for a few miles. Then my daughter yelled, "He's looking at me," and my son replied, "Well, she's looking at me." Before we even arrived at the amusement park, I knew we were doomed.

The day went from bad to worse. Even as we entered the amusement park gate, they began to complain. Why couldn't we buy them souvenirs? Why did we have to eat pizza for lunch instead of hamburgers? Why did we ride the attraction my daughter wanted to ride before we rode the one my son wanted? Why did we have to stand in line?

I finally lost it in the line for the Tilt-A-Whirl. My son was hanging on the bars dividing our line from the next when he slipped and fell. My daughter laughed. More embarrassed than hurt, my son screamed, "I hate you!" My daughter stuck out her tongue and said, "I hate you too." I snapped. I yanked them out of the line, sat them down on the nearest bench, and began my tirade.

"You are the most ungrateful children in the world. Your mother and I have worked our fingers to the bone saving money for months for this trip, and you two have ruined it. You have fought ever since we got in the car. You have complained about everything we've done. You have treated each other horribly. We are going home, and we are never coming back here again. In fact, we're never taking you anywhere again. You are going to spend the rest of your lives in your rooms."

Nothing hurts a parent more than ingratitude.

My gifts to my children are freely given. My sole motivation is my love for them. Yet I always hope my gifts will produce gratitude. Thomas Merton said, "Unselfish love that is poured out upon a selfish object does not bring perfect happiness: not because love requires a return or a reward for loving, but because it rests in the happiness of the beloved. And if the one loved receives love selfishly, the lover is not satisfied."[1] What is true of human love is equally true with divine love.

Gratitude and Grace

Jesus told a story of gratitude and grace. He spoke of a man who owed a king millions of dollars. His debt came due, and he was brought before the throne. He couldn't pay the debt and begged for mercy. He asked for more time. Instead, the king forgave the entire debt. It was an unexpected act of grace.

The story doesn't end there. The forgiven man left the king's presence and came across another man who owed him a few dollars. He demanded payment. That man also pled for mercy, but the first man refused. He had his debtor thrown into prison.

Soon the king heard of this outrage and called the first man to account. He said, "You wicked servant! I canceled all that debt of yours because you begged me to. Shouldn't you have had mercy on your fellow servant just as I had on you? Throw this man in jail to be tortured and don't let him out until he pays every single penny he owes!"

Jesus said, "This is how my Father in heaven will treat each of you unless you forgive your brother from your heart" (Matt. 18:32–35).

Nothing hurts God more than ingratitude. It is always evidence of our selfishness. We have pleaded for our Father's mercy without accepting the responsibility to forgive our brothers and sisters. How can God be happy when he knows our hearts have yet to be transformed? God is never satisfied until we love as he loves. The proper response to love is gratitude. It is gratitude that creates grace. When we live without gratitude, we find it impossible to act with grace.

Why should we be grateful? Life is reason enough. I never attend an African American worship service without hearing someone pray, "God, thank you for getting me up this morning. Thank you for letting me take another breath." The first time I heard such a prayer I thought it strange. I took getting up and breathing for granted. The more I thought about my attitude, the more I realized it was my lack of gratitude that was odd. Perhaps it is those who have had the least who are most aware of the goodness of God.

A few years ago, Victoria entered our lives. She was our

daughter's best friend and became a daughter to us. Victoria had a horrible childhood. She was abused by her father, abandoned by her mother, and passed from relative to relative. Somehow she still got good grades, had the lead in the school play, and graduated with honors. It was a great joy to include her in our family.

Whenever we did anything for her, no matter how minor, she would thank us. I told my own children they could learn from Victoria. They seldom thanked me for my goodness to them. Of course, I often forget to thank God for his goodness to me. Knowing Victoria has reminded me of my blessings—good parents, a supportive family, and a safe home. These are not small gifts. Given Victoria's circumstances, I wonder if I would have done as well.

Victoria also taught me that God's goodness and grace have a purpose. They should enable me to be merciful to the Victorias of the world—those who overcome their circumstances, and those who don't. The more I am aware of God's goodness to me, the more I am able to be gracious to those around me.

One day, Jesus had dinner with some tax collectors and other sinners. The Pharisees saw this and were indignant. They said, "Why does your teacher eat with people like that?" On hearing this, Jesus said, "It is not the healthy who need a doctor, but the sick. Go and learn what this means: 'I desire mercy, not sacrifice'" (Matt. 9:10–13).

The desire of God is not judgment, condemnation, or punishment. No parent finds any joy in these acts. What a parent hopes for is repentance, reconciliation, and mercy. Even when we speak harsh words to our children, we are hoping to confront them with their ingratitude and move them toward grace.

You need to know how our trip to the amusement park ended. On the way home, there was no touching, looking at each other, or fighting. The only noise was my son and daughter whispering. Finally, my daughter said, "Daddy, we're sorry."

My son immediately added, "I'm sorry too, Daddy."

For the first time that day, I smiled. My children didn't spend the rest of their lives in their rooms. We went back to the amusement park the next summer. We had a great time.

I think the story Jesus told of the ungrateful servant is incomplete. It ends with the king throwing the man in the jail to be tortured until he pays his debt. I recognize that threat. It sounds remarkably similar to my threat that my children would spend the rest of their lives in their rooms. Jail and torture can't be the end of the story. A king might be satisfied with such an ending, but a father would know it to be an idle threat. So would a child.

I think the ungrateful servant sat in his jail cell and realized that the king desired mercy. I suspect he called for the jailer and asked to see the king once again. I believe the king granted his wish. After all, he is the one who commanded his servants to be gracious. When the man stood before the king once again, he said, "I'm sorry. I will forgive my debtors as you have forgiven me." I imagine the king, whose greatest desire is for his children to learn to be merciful, smiled.

Grace has a dual purpose. It is intended to restore us to a proper relationship to God. We are forgiven so we can climb into God's lap without fear or guilt. Grace is also intended to restore us to a proper relationship with one another. God's desire is to see his children reconciled with one another.

This was my hope for our trip to the amusement park. I didn't need my children to constantly thank me for saving money, buying the tickets, and taking them there. Seeing them be good to each other would have been thanks enough. Nothing pleases parents more than watching their children play happily together.

Revenge or Reconciliation?

I am not the only one to take my children on trips. God took the children of Israel on a journey to a promised land. Unfortunately, his experience with his children was as unpleasant as mine. Micah was one of the prophets who finally lost patience with the children of Israel, yanked them out of line, and scolded them for how they were acting.

He reminded them of God's goodness to them—how God had rescued them from slavery in Egypt, sustained them in the wilderness, and brought them to a land flowing with milk and honey. And how had they responded to God's grace? They had rewarded God's faithfulness with rebellion, with violence toward one another, and with ingratitude. Micah told them they had hurt God.

He also told them what God expected. "He has showed you, O man, what is good. And what does the Lord require of you? To act justly, to love mercy, and to walk humbly with your God" (Mic. 6:8). Mercy is a message we need to hear repeatedly. Jesus said, "Be merciful, just as your Father is merciful" (Luke 6:36). The church proclaimed, "Mercy triumphs over judgment" (James 2:13). The requirement for mercy runs through Scripture from beginning to end.

"Forgive us our sins, as we forgive those who sin against us" is one more call to mercy. Forgiveness is not optional. It is the foundation of a healthy relationship with God and with others. To love mercy is to be like God and to love others as God loves them.

I do not love mercy. Too often, I approach mercy as a requirement rather than a joy. I don't like it, but if God insists, I'll try. It seems so unnatural. I love judgment. An eye for an eye and a tooth for a tooth. What goes around comes around. Someday they'll get what they deserve. Those are the phrases that trip so easily off my tongue. "I forgive you" sticks to the roof of my mouth.

I love revenge fantasies. Someone cuts me off in traffic and has the audacity to glare at me. Immediately, my imagination kicks in. I fantasize that a few blocks later I see them getting out of their smashed car or pulled over by the police. I salute them as I slowly drive by. I have trouble resisting road rage. I can only imagine my struggle if someone really sinned against me.

Bud Welch's daughter, Julie, was killed in the Oklahoma City federal building bombing. When he heard of Timothy McVeigh's arrest, he felt only rage and a desire for vengeance. McVeigh's lack of repentance only made his anger hotter. He said, "I just wanted him fried."

Bud's hate took him on a journey of sleepless nights and drunken binges to numb the pain. It is also lead him to visit the bombing site. On that visit, he vowed to change. He remembered watching Bill McVeigh, the bomber's father, on television and suddenly recognizing his pain and grief in that father's eyes.

He arranged to meet Bill McVeigh. They sat together and talked about their children, one who was dead and one who soon would be. Forgiveness and mercy overwhelmed Bud Welch. He said, "I never felt closer to God than I did at that moment." When asked later about those who resented his forgiveness of Timothy McVeigh, he said, "They think they'll get some kind of healing. There's nothing about killing that's going to help them."

Revenge never solves anything. The cycles of violence in Northern Ireland, Israel, Bosnia, and Rwanda witness to a cross-cultural commitment to revenge. Generations of death and misery also testify to revenge's impotence. Mercy, forgiveness, and reconciliation are far more than personal issues. When societies fail to value these acts, the fabric of human interaction is torn. We begin to relate to one another from the least common denominator—hate.

Although grace is a vital dynamic in our personal lives, it is also the intention of God for the kingdoms of this world. "In the last days, the mountain of the Lord's temple will be established as chief among the mountains; it will be raised above the hills, and all nations will stream to it. . . . They will beat their swords into plowshares and their spears into pruning hooks. Nation will not take up sword against nation, nor will they train for war anymore" (Isa. 2:2–4). This image of the last days is a far cry from the popular Christian expectation of Armageddon, judgment, and the pits of hell. It implies reconciliation rather than revenge. It suggests Christians should oppose rather than tolerate the industries of war.

What displeases God is when his children fight. He is disappointed when we carefully draw dividing lines and refuse to touch or be touched by those on the other side. He grows weary of our selfish complaints. He is discouraged by our demands to have more than our brothers and sisters. When we begin to scream our hate for one another at the slightest offense, we try God's patience and rebel against his will. We sadden our Father in heaven.

When in our personal and international interactions we choose judgment over mercy and revenge over reconciliation, we thwart the will of God and postpone the establishment of God's kingdom. Revenge fantasies do great damage when they become national policy. After World War I, the Allies chose revenge and demanded reparation as their response to German aggression. This contributed to bringing about Adolf Hitler, the Holocaust, and millions of deaths less than twenty years later.

Fortunately, in part because of the wisdom of Harry Truman, the response of the Allies to Germany and Japan's defeat in World War II was reconciliation instead of revenge. The Marshall Plan sought to restore families, cities, and countries. Some would argue that the battles at Normandy or Iwo Jima were the most courageous acts of the war. I believe it was the mercy we extended to our enemies after the war.

Abraham Lincoln set an example of such mercy at the end of the Civil War. Many were arguing for swift and terrible retribution upon the South. They wanted their enemies destroyed. Lincoln asked, "Do I not destroy my enemy when I make him my friend?" Lincoln believed what the Bible teaches—mercy triumphs over judgment.

Paul said, "If anyone is in Christ, they are a new creation; the old is gone and the new has come! All this is from God, who reconciled us to himself through Christ and gave us the ministry of reconciliation: that God was reconciling the world to himself in Christ, not counting men's sins against them. And he has committed to us the message of reconciliation" (2 Cor. 5:17–19). If God is committed to this message, shouldn't his children be too?

I've tried in the past few years to begin having reconciliation fantasies. Someone cuts me off in traffic and then glares at me. A few blocks later I see them pulled over at the side of the road with a flat tire. I stop and ask if I can help them. We change the tire, and I discover they've been having a rough week. We talk together, and I ask if I can pray for them. We shake hands as I turn to go.

This may seem a silly exercise, but I do it in preparation for the greater challenges of mercy. The sins against me may not always be so minor. I want to believe I could do what Bud Welch did, but I'm not certain. I am sure of this—my ability to be merciful is directly connected to my awareness of God's mercy toward me. Only when I recognize God's goodness and grace am I able to seek reconciliation rather than revenge. I so easily forget to be grateful. I'm like my children at the amusement park. I take the goodness of God for granted. I complain about even the minor things. I get upset when things don't go exactly my way. When life will not bend to my will, I act like a selfish child.

When we pray to our Father and seek his mercy, we are always forgiven. Yet Jesus understood our tendency to celebrate God's mercy even while being unmerciful. It would have been challenging enough if Jesus had simply said, "Forgive us our sins." But then Jesus added the word "as." The Greek word can be translated "in proportion to." He was saying, "Forgive us in the same manner as we forgive others." You can't pray those words without examining your life. They expose the deficiencies in the measures we use for forgiveness.

The Measures of Grace

Brian was a jerk. Everyone at our small college thought so. He was rude and mean. Unfortunately, Brian and I shared the same major and had many classes and activities together. This meant I experienced his "jerkness" more often than others.

I was quick to report these incidents to my friends. They would shake their heads as I told another story of Brian's selfishness. Then they would share their own tales of his misbehavior. We could spend a whole evening talking about Brian. And the more we talked about him, the less I liked him.

One morning I was having devotions when I read these words of Jesus: "Do not judge, and you will not be judged. Do not condemn, and you will not be condemned. Forgive, and you will be forgiven. Give, and it will be given to you. A good measure, pressed down, shaken together and running over, will be poured into your lap. For with the measure you use, it will be measured to you" (Luke 6:37–38).

I immediately thought about Brian. I had judged him and found him wanting. I had condemned him and become his enemy. I had been unwilling to forgive him. The Holy Spirit challenged my attitude toward Brian. I had been demanding Brian repent even as I sinned against him.

Self-righteousness is a seductive sin. When I glory in my goodness, the sins of others seem more heinous. When I forget my need for forgiveness, the sins of others are more difficult to forgive. When I pray, "Forgive us our sins," I acknowledge I have something in common with even my worst enemy: we both need forgiveness.

The afternoon after my devotional epiphany, I called Brian and asked if we could meet at the student union. I told him I needed to talk with him. He sounded suspicious, but he agreed to meet. We sat down and I began to talk.

I said, "Brian, I need to ask your forgiveness. I've been talking about you behind you back. You've done some things to upset me, but that doesn't excuse the things I've said. I'm sorry."

Now I had imagined that at this point Brian would be moved and humbled by my apology and respond, "Gee, I'm sorry too. I have been a rude, mean person. Would you please forgive me?"

Instead, Brian said, "I am really disappointed in you. It is really rude and mean to talk behind someone's back. I thought you were a Christian. I'm very hurt, but I'll try to forgive you." Then he got up and walked away.

I thought, "What a jerk!"

As I sat there stunned and disappointed, I realized how difficult forgiveness is, especially when the person we are trying to forgive doesn't repent. I was willing to apologize for my gossip. I was willing to forgive Brian for his behavior. I was willing to do these things as long as he repented. Instead of repenting, he'd given me one more reason to dislike him.

I immediately went and told my friends what he had said. I justified my behavior. If he wouldn't repent of his meanness, then why should I repent of my gossip? Of course, this was opposite of what Jesus taught. I had exchanged "forgive us our sins, as we forgive those who sin against us" for "sin against others, as they have sinned against you."

"Forgive us our sins, as we forgive those who sin against us" is such a clever phrase. In one sentence, it reminds us of so much. We have sinned against others. We need forgiveness. Others have sinned against us. They need forgiveness. Our Father is a forgiving God. We need to be as forgiving. The Prayer of Jesus asks this question: Do we want God's forgiveness to be diminished or our mercy to be expanded? Do we want God to use human measures?

There is the eyedropper of forgiveness. We say, "When you repent on bent knee, admit it was all your fault, and finally accept that I am better than you, I will forgive you. Now open your eyes because this is going to sting."

There is the teaspoon of forgiveness. We say, "I'll forgive you, but I'll never forget what you did. In fact, I'll probably remind you of your sin nearly every day. Now open you mouth and take your medicine."

There is the cup of forgiveness. We say, "I'll forgive you this time, but never again. I'm going to watch you like a hawk because I don't really believe you've repented. Drink up and don't mind the bitterness."

There is the cup of forgiveness with two straws. We say, "I'm sorry for what I did as long as you're sorry for what you did. I'll stop my sin if you stop yours." That was the measure of forgiveness I offered Brian.

The problem with all these measures of forgiveness is that

they fail to measure up to the grace of God. When we pray "forgive us our sins, as we forgive those who sin against us," we realize the conditions and limits of human forgiveness. We are also reminded of the unconditional and limitless grace of God.

One day, Peter came to Jesus and asked, "Lord, how many times shall I forgive my brother when he sins against me? Up to seven times?" (Matt. 18:21). Peter was trying to impress the Lord. Seven times seemed extravagant to him.

Jesus answered, "I tell you, not seven times, but seventy times seven" (v. 22).

Of course, Jesus was not suggesting that 490 should be the limit of our forgiveness or of God's. Indeed, Jesus went on to tell that story of the king who forgave a man his debt of millions—the same man who was then unmerciful toward another who owed him a few dollars. This is another reason I am convinced the ungrateful and wicked man got a second chance. Jesus told his story to illustrate the infinite grace of God. The forgiveness Jesus described was not limited to an eyedropper or a teaspoon or even a cup with two straws. The forgiveness of God is poured from a bottomless bucket.

Paul said, "God has poured out his love into our hearts. God demonstrates his own love for us in this: while we were yet sinners, Christ died for us" (Rom. 5:5, 8). Jesus said, "A good measure, pressed down, shaken together and running over, will be poured into your lap" (Luke 6:38). God's grace is not given in response to our repentance, but in anticipation of it. While we were yet sinners, before we had repented, God began to pour out his buckets of forgiveness. God says, "You are loved. Let me pour my grace over your head and allow it to run down your shoulders. Allow my mercy to refresh and renew and cleanse."

This is the measure God uses. When we pray, "Forgive us our sins, as we forgive those who sin against us," we are praying a prayer of proportion. Do we want God to come down to our level or are we pledging to rise to his? Do we want heaven to be as it is on earth or do we want earth to be as it is in heaven?

What measure do we want God to use when we stand before his throne? Do we want him to use the measures we've applied to others? Or do we yearn for his infinite grace? When I remember that those who were naked and without shelter, sick and oppressed, starving and dying of thirst will also stand before that throne, I hope for buckets of forgiveness from God and from them.

When I remember that Brian will be there, I want to apologize again, not for my gossip or arrogance, but for my lack of love. I want seek forgiveness for my unwillingness to befriend my enemy, to love a jerk, to care for the selfish, to reach out to one who pushed me away. We err when we understand forgiveness as our gift. Grace never begins in us. It is always a response to the One who has delivered us from the evil of this world and, more important, from the evil within ourselves.

1. Thomas Merton, *No Man Is an Island* (Harvest/Harcourt Brace Jovanovich, 1955), p. 3. This is an excerpt from an essay entitled "Love Can Be Kept Only by Being Given Away." It may be one of the finest essays on love ever written.

SIX

~ ⌒

Deliver Us

Lead us not into temptation, but deliver us from evil.

I remember vividly the day Jim Bakker, television evangelist and prophet of prosperity theology, was convicted of fraud and sentenced to forty-four years in prison. It was October 6, 1989. It was my birthday. I considered his conviction a wonderful gift.

I had no sympathy for him or his family. I thought he was a charlatan who had bilked millions from the people who had watched his television program. I had always distanced my Christianity as far as possible from the religion he promoted. When he was hauled off to prison, I said, "Good riddance."

Several years later I walked into a library and saw his face on the cover of a book. He had written an autobiography entitled *I Was Wrong.* It chronicled his downfall, his five years in prison, and an amazing transformation. He wrote, "God does not promise that we will all be rich and prosperous, as I once preached. When I finally studied the Bible while in prison, it became clear to me that not one man or woman—not even the prophets of God—led a life without pain."[1] Painful personal reflection led him to admit, "I was wrong."

His confession sparked my self-examination. I realized I too was wrong. I had quickly and easily judged and condemned him. As I read his story, he sounded remarkably like me. He was a man of humble beginnings and grand dreams. He was a person committed to God and driven to serve. He was a man who allowed his obsessions to consume him.

I had wanted to believe Jim Bakker an aberration. I was wrong. His glaring greed and religious justifications were merely the symptoms of a much wider epidemic. Millions watched his television program because they wanted his message to be true. We prosecuted Jim Bakker, but ignored the question of why thousands of people, when promised blessing, sent him checks.

Bakker confessed to "the temptation to have more, do more, earn more, build bigger, emphasize material things rather than spiritual, protect the image regardless of cost, look the other way rather than confront wrongs."[2] When I read those words, I recognized them as a good description of American Christianity. More frightening, those words could easily describe my life.

This obsession with material blessing, at the expense of the spiritual, is a congenital disease. Being born an American is to be so afflicted. Jim Bakker was merely the most blatant prophet of a philosophy to which most of us pledge allegiance. His lifestyle was an exaggeration of a nearly universal merger of religious life and the predominant values of our culture. He sprinkled holy water on the American way.

Of course, greed wrapped in a flag and holding a Bible is still greed. Avarice as a national policy with a religious mandate is an evil of grand proportion. It is this evil from which we need deliverance. Such evil is far more dangerous than the personal temptations we face each day. It is far more subtle than the personal sins we often confess. The kingdom of God, with its equality of blessing, cannot come as long as a majority of us ignore our complicity in the inequalities.

"Lead us not into temptation, but deliver us from evil" is not a personal mantra for protection. It is recognition of our tendency to march lockstep into sins with great social and global implications. When we fail to emphasize our corporate need for deliverance, we make the closing words of the Prayer of Jesus into another selfish petition.

Though there are many temptations in our lives, when the prosperous seek deliverance we are asking to be delivered from the temptations of wealth. The Bible warns, "People who want to get rich fall into temptation and a trap and into many foolish and harmful desires that plunge men into ruin and destruction. For the love of money is a root of all kinds of evil" (1 Tim. 6:9–10). Getting rich is the American dream. Personal prosperity is the great American temptation.

The Great American Temptation

Jim Bakker said, "To my surprise, after months of studying Jesus, I concluded that He did not have one good thing to say about money."[3] In fact, Jesus thought money the most tempting alternative to God. He said, "No one can serve two masters. Either he will hate the one and love the other, or he will be devoted to the one and despise the other. You cannot serve both God and Money" (Matt. 6:24). Jesus warned his disciples of many temptations and traps, but he gave only money the status of a god.

Unfortunately, most of us seem convinced we can balance our commitment to God with our desire for affluence. Even when we acknowledge its temptation, we pretend to be free of its power. I have often preached that the love of money, and not money itself, is the root of all kinds of evil. Although this was a valid point, my lifestyle suggested I was deceiving myself. I did not want to admit how easily money could entice and drag me away.

In the Parable of the Sower, Jesus explained what happened when people heard of the kingdom of God. Some heard the message and it never took root. In others, it took root until trouble and persecution came; then it withered away. In still others, the message thrived; it was ready to produce fruit. Jesus said, "But the worries of this life and the deceitfulness of wealth choke it, making it unfruitful" (Matt. 13:22).

A life centered in personal prosperity and material blessing is a life built on a lie. Jim Bakker discovered that when his life was stripped of pretense and justification, all that remained was the ugly truth. He had worshiped an idol of silver and gold. The truth is that much of the church, whether actively promoting prosperity theology or not, has bowed down before that same idol. We believe a false doctrine. We are those "who have been robbed of the truth and who think that godliness is a means to financial gain" (1 Tim. 6:5).

The message of Jesus concerning money is one we don't want to hear. We want to believe his words are aimed at someone else. The rich are the millionaires and billionaires. They are the ones who love money. As long as there is someone more extravagant than we are, we justify our affluence. We fail to recognize they simply have more of what we want.

We all want more. Jesus commanded less. He said, "Do not be afraid, little flock, for your Father has been pleased to give you the kingdom. Sell your possessions and give to the poor. Provide purses for yourselves that will not wear out, a treasure in heaven that will not be exhausted, where no thief comes near and no moth destroys. For where your treasure is, there your heart will be also" (Luke 12:32–34).

I remember my anger when a thief broke into our home and stole some of our possessions. Several people called to sympathize. One of them asked, "Don't you feel violated?" I thought about that question. What does it say about us when we value material things so much that we consider their theft a violation? The deeper question is whether we own our possessions or our possessions own us. The only sure way to know the answer is to have them taken away.

Perhaps this is why Jesus said, "Give to everyone who asks you, and if anyone takes what belongs to you, do not demand it back" (Luke 6:30). Jesus wasn't encouraging theft. He was discouraging us from attaching too much value to objects. He knew our temptation to focus our life around the attainment of flat, round pieces of metal. We call them coins, stamp them with the motto "In God We Trust," and are oblivious to the irony. Is the god in whom we trust the God of Jesus or the money jingling in our pockets?

We all want to earn more. Jesus commanded us to give

more away. One day, Jesus was watching people bring their gifts to the Temple treasury. He saw a poor widow put in two small copper coins. He said, "I tell you the truth, this poor widow has put in more than all the others. All these people gave their gifts out of their wealth; but she out of her poverty put in all she had to live on" (Luke 21:3–4).

Bishop Fulton Sheen said, "Generosity is not measured by how much you give. It is measured by how much you have left." When we focus on earning more, we seldom give more. There is actually a decline in the percentage of giving as we become wealthier. My most prosperous parishioners are seldom the most generous.

This compulsion to earn more does damage to our marriages, families, churches, and the world. The evidence is stark. One of the top four reasons for divorce is money. We are committed to lifestyles that demand two incomes and deep debt. We pass each other on the way to our jobs. We have abandoned our children to day care and traded our leisure for overtime. We have defined the successful church as the one with the biggest attendance and budget. We have made acquiring wealth a higher priority than caring for the needs of starving people. Although I understand greed is not our only problem, I suspect much of the pain in our lives, marriages, families, churches, and world would be eliminated if we were to acknowledge its power.

We all believe "bigger is better." Jesus commanded us to build better relationships rather than bigger personal kingdoms. He said, "I tell you, use worldly wealth to gain friends for yourselves, so when it is gone, you will be welcomed into eternal dwellings" (Luke 16:9). The proper use of wealth is to strengthen our relationships.

A bigger house, a fancier car, a fatter stock portfolio, a larger business, and a more influential ministry are not the goals of God. Jim Bakker said, "As with so many things done under my leadership at PTL, we started with the best of intentions and somehow got sidetracked onto a path of pride, arrogance and indulgence. We got trapped in the subtle snare that says, 'big is better.'"[4] While Jim Bakker's ministry and bank account were expanding, his marriage, his family, and his own emotional and spiritual health were disintegrating.

Though I have never achieved Jim Bakker's prominence, I have twice sacrificed my own health, marriage, and family in order to expand a ministry. Each time I convinced myself that God wanted what I wanted. Fortunately, in both instances, God finally broke through my fixation on the visible and showed me the invisible. Though I was visibly prosperous, my emphasis on the symbols of success had drained my spirit.

We all emphasize the material. Jesus emphasized the spiritual. He said, "What good will it be for a man if he gains the whole world, yet forfeits his soul? Or what can a man give in exchange for his soul?" (Matt. 16:26). In our culture, far too many of us have exchanged our souls for silver and gold. We have confused the riches of the kingdom of God with the wealth of this world.

This obsession is apparent whenever a group of pastors gathers. One pastor will ask another, "How is your church doing?" The other pastor will almost always respond with attendance and financial figures. We measure the health of the church on the scales of prosperity. We are unconscious of our compromises.

There is no clearer indication of our confusion than the way we celebrate the Christmas holiday. We have taken the birth of Christ, a moment with tremendous spiritual meaning, and made it into the biggest commercial event of the year. We celebrate the gift of a relationship—our relationship to God through Jesus—by buying each other gifts we do not need. We waste enough money during one month to meet the real needs of the entire world. We spend far more time during the Christmas season in the malls, the "cathedrals" of commerce, than we do in our churches.

If we have not been trustworthy in handling the world's wealth, how can we be trusted with spiritual riches? Jesus said, "Whoever can be trusted with very little can also be trusted with much, and whoever is dishonest with very little will also be dishonest with much. So if you have not been trustworthy in handling worldly wealth, who will trust you with true riches" (Luke 16:10–11). The kingdom of God will advance, but if the American church chooses material prosperity, it will forfeit the opportunity to be spiritually rich. We may retain the title of the wealthiest country in the world, but we will miss the vast spiritual blessing of the kingdom of God.

We all protect our image of prosperity so carefully. Yet Jesus called us to service. He said, "The greatest among you will be your servant. For whoever exalts himself will be humbled and whoever humbles himself will be exalted" (Matt. 23:11–12).

The disciples of Jesus always resisted this call. One day Jesus grew so frustrated with them that he took off his outer clothes, poured some water in a basin, and began to wash his disciples' feet. This was a task usually reserved for the lowest of servants. When he was finished he asked, "Do you understand what I have done for you? You call me 'Teacher' and 'Lord,' and rightly so, for that is what I am. Now that I, your Lord and Teacher, have washed your feet, you should also wash one another's feet. I have set you an example so that you should do as I have done for you" (John 13:12–15).

What would happen in the American church if we washed each other's feet as often as we took Communion? Isn't it revealing how readily we adopt those acts that celebrate what God has done for us and resist those acts that represent our responsibility to serve one another? What would it mean if washing the dirty feet of the world became our commitment and joy?

The great American temptation is to want more, earn more, to seek bigger and better things, to emphasize the material at the expense of the spiritual, and to protect our image of prosperity at any cost. Yet God offers us far more than prosperity. God offers us a kingdom rich in blessings, blessings that cannot be measured in dollars.

We cannot serve two masters. The cost is too high. We must decide what we treasure most: the things of man or the things of God. Jesus said, "The kingdom of heaven is like treasure hidden in a field. When a man found it, he hid it again, and then in his joy sold all he had and bought that field" (Matt. 13:44). It is the kingdom of God that is worth the cost. Until we are tempted by nothing less than living in the kingdom of God, we will be slaves to prosperity.

Jesus reminded his disciples that God is "Our Father" and we are brothers and sisters. He asked us to commit ourselves to God's kingdom and will. He commanded us to give and forgive. But I believe what will change our lives, and ultimately transform the world, is to acknowledge the temptations of silver and gold, to confess our desire for and dependence upon material wealth, and to be delivered from our lust for more.

Confession

He stood and said, "I'm Bob and I'm an alcoholic."

I heard Bob speak at an AA meeting in our church basement. The group met on Saturdays at midnight. I thought that an odd hour to meet until they explained it was their time of greatest temptation. It was when they used to hit the bars.

Bob went on to say, "Every morning I wake up knowing I am only one drink away from destroying my life again. When I was drinking, I lost my family, my job, my health, and my self-respect. God has given me those gifts back, but I realize it takes only one drink for me to lose those treasures again. I wish I could say I didn't want that drink, but I do. Every day I am tempted—some days more than others. Every day I have to make the right choice. Only by the grace of God can I remain sober."

I was deeply moved by Bob's honesty and the similar confessions of others in his group. As I listened, I heard something I seldom heard in the church—honesty. Confession may be good for the soul, but it is rare in the church. We have exchanged honesty for pretense. We come to worship with our struggles safely hidden. We dress in our finest clothes, talk in the noblest terms, and act happy. Acting is an important skill for many church members. We act as if we've seen no evil, heard no evil, and done no evil. We greet each other with, "How are you?" and respond with, "Blessed." Too often that is a lie.

Confessing our struggle is the first of what alcoholics call the "twelve steps." The first step is "to admit you are powerless over alcohol and that your life has become unmanageable." Those words sound like the whispered admissions I've heard at church altars from countless broken persons. Often the struggle isn't alcohol. It can be sexual immorality, drug addiction, abusive behavior, stealing, or lying. These are "acceptable" struggles. I have yet to have someone come to the altar or visit me in my office and confess, "I'm greedy."

Our inability to confess our greatest temptation indicates how powerless we are over our love of money and how our lives have become unmanageable. Yet only in confessing our struggle can we hope for deliverance. "If we claim to be without sin, we deceive ourselves and the truth is not in us. If we confess our sins, God is faithful and just and will forgive our sins and purify us from all unrighteousness" (1 John 1:8–9). Without confession, we remain slaves to our temptations and sins.

What would happen if American church services became meetings of "Avarice Anonymous"? What if we abandoned our crystal cathedrals and began meeting in homes, basements, schools, and backyards? What if we began our worship services by confessing, "I'm Jim and I'm greedy"? Attendance might decrease, but I suspect spiritual health would skyrocket.

I can imagine the testimonies. "Every morning I wake up knowing greed can destroy my life. My greed can cause me to ignore my family, worship my job, destroy my health, and define my worth in dollars. I wish I could say I don't depend on money, but I do. My credit cards, savings accounts, stocks and bonds, pensions, and insurance policies are my security. Every day I want more and more. Only by the grace of God can I be delivered from this insanity."

In the twelve steps, the second step is "to believe that a power greater than ourselves could restore us to sanity." This is our hope when we pray, "Lead us not into temptation, but deliver us from evil."

When the rich young ruler went away sad because of his great wealth, Jesus said, "I tell you the truth, it is hard for a rich man to enter the kingdom of heaven."

When the disciples heard this, they were greatly astonished and asked, "Who then can be saved?"

Jesus looked at them and said, "With man this is impossible, but with God all things are possible" (Matt. 19:22–26). Only God can deliver us from our love of money.

The third step is "to make a decision to turn our will and lives over to the care of God as we understand him." This is the final battle of the spiritual journey. It is the slow and painful task of uniting our will with the will of God. Once we have confessed the power of prosperity to turn our eyes from God, abandoned our justifications and excuses for seeking after more, acknowledged our temptation to worship at the altar of avarice, only then can God begin to transform us from self-centered creatures into the gracious men and women we were intended to be.

Jim Bakker said, "In retrospect, one of the main reasons I slipped into believing and preaching a distorted doctrine was because of my lack of understanding of what it really means to allow Jesus to be Lord of your life. I had accepted Jesus as my Savior and with my lips I had called Him 'Lord,' but in my heart and lifestyle, I now realized that He was not the Lord of my life; I was."[5] In the end, we are delivered from temptation and evil when we surrender our lives to God.

Deliverance

Confessing the temptation of prosperity is the first and most difficult step toward spiritual health. It will always humble us. In admitting our love of money, we become conscious of the ugliness of greed. In acknowledging our infatuation with wealth, we can more easily see how it ensnares us. In confessing we have too much, we are freed to live on so much less. Once we are honest, prosperity begins to lose its power to entice and destroy.

Temptation becomes the tool of God to transform and empower us to establish his kingdom in the world. The allure of affluence becomes a constant reminder of what is really important to God. Jim Bakker humbly admitted he was wrong. In so doing, he was freed to finally focus on the priorities of God. The saints are not those who are no longer tempted. The saints are those who have seen enough of the kingdom of God to be able to resist the kingdoms of this world. This is what happened when Jesus was tempted in the wilderness.

We forget Jesus was tempted. Indeed, before the Bible reports his teachings, his miracles, his healings, and his acts of goodness and grace, it tells of his temptations. Have you ever wondered how we know of the temptations of Jesus? Obviously, no one was there with him. He was alone in the wilderness for forty days and forty nights. He didn't have to tell anyone of his struggle. He could have kept his image pristine. Apparently, Jesus thought his disciples needed to know of his temptations.

I can almost imagine that night around the campfire. Perhaps it was after some triumph—the healing of a leper, the exorcism of a demon, or his walking on the water. I'm sure the disciples were all marveling at his power. I can hear

Peter saying, "You are the Messiah, the son of the living God." In this moment of adoration, I can hear Jesus saying, "Let me tell you about my temptations."

His first temptation was to use his power, gifts, and resources in his own self-interest. He was hungry after forty days of fasting. Temptation said, "If you are the Son of God, turn these stones into bread." He was tempted to focus on his needs rather than on the kingdom of God. Then Jesus remembered, "It is written, 'Man does not live on bread alone, but on every word that comes from the mouth of God'" (Matt. 4:4). There is far more to life than prosperity.

His second temptation was to use his power, gifts, and resources for self-advancement. Temptation said, "If you are the Son of God, throw yourself down off the temple and the angels will catch you." He was tempted to use his relationship with God for his own blessing. Then Jesus remembered, "It is also written, 'Do not put the Lord your God to the test'" (Matt. 4:7). There is far more to life than fame.

His final temptation was to use his power, gifts, and resources to succeed in the kingdoms of this world. Temptation said, "All the kingdoms of the world I will give you, if you will bow down and worship me." He was tempted with everything other than the kingdom of God. Then Jesus remembered, "It is written, 'Worship the Lord your God, and serve him only'" (Matt. 4:10). There is far more to life than success.

Jesus refused to be satisfied with anything less than God's kingdom. Each of his responses reminds us of the priorities of God. "Lead us not into temptation" is a cry for the strength to resist the seductiveness of wealth. When coupled with the plea "Deliver us from evil," it is the commitment to challenge the kingdoms of this world, even those we have been born into and that entice us each day.

Paul said, "No temptation has seized you except what is common to man. And God is faithful; he will not let you be tempted beyond what you can bear. But when you are tempted, he will also provide a way out so that you can stand up under it" (1 Cor. 10:13). There is a way out of the materialistic wilderness in which we have lived for so long.

We must follow Jesus. It was only after Jesus had triumphed over his temptations that he began his ministry. It was a ministry that changed the world. It was the proclamation of the kingdom whose riches exceed all the silver and gold. We who follow Jesus have accepted his call and joined him in establishing this kingdom. Jesus said, "I tell you the truth, anyone who has faith in me will do what I have been doing. He will do even greater things than these" (John 14:12).

We too can do great things. We can live as children of God. We can establish God's kingdom and do his will. We can give generously to the needy. We can forgive those who sin against us. We can abandon our love of money and be delivered from our obsession with personal prosperity. We can finally be free to be the people of God.

1. Jim Bakker, *I Was Wrong* (Thomas Nelson, 1996), p. xiii.

2. Ibid., p. xiv.

3. Ibid., p. 531.

4. Ibid., p. 465.

5. Ibid., p. 543.

~ ~

SEVEN

A Final Word:

Amen

For thine is the kingdom and the power and the glory forever.
Amen.

The Prayer of Jesus closes with the words "Deliver us from evil." It is a fitting end. Jesus had defined our relationship to God and each other, and challenged us to establish God's kingdom and accomplish God's will. He had outlined our responsibility to give and forgive, and reminded us of the temptations of this world and God's ability to deliver us from their clutches. The final phrase of the prayer that we repeat in worship, "For thine is the kingdom and the power and the glory forever," was probably a later addition.

None of the earliest biblical manuscripts include the closing refrain. It may have been a device used by early Christians in affirmation of the Prayer of Jesus. They would have been borrowing from the common Jewish pattern of benediction and assent. The benediction acknowledged God's kingdom, power, and glory. It reminds us of God's presence and power as we endeavor to live out the Prayer of Jesus.

Even more important was the addition of "Amen." In most churches, this word has degenerated into a signal that a prayer is over and we can all lift our heads. In the Jewish tradition, it was much more meaningful. It literally meant, "So be it." It was the worshipers' commitment to do what they had prayed. It was a vow.

I remember when I stood next to my wife on our wedding day. The minister asked, "Do you, Jim, take Angie to be your wife, to have and to hold from this day forward, for better for worse, for richer for poorer, in sickness and in health, to love and to cherish, until parted by death?" I answered, "I do."

The more I repeat the Prayer of Jesus, the more it reminds me of that vow. Saying "I do" was not the end of my commitment, but the beginning. I was pledging to fulfill those words—to have and to hold, for better or worse, for richer for poorer, in sickness and in health, to love and to cherish—in the years ahead. That has not always been easy, but in keeping that vow there has been blessing.

When we say "Amen," we are not finishing a list of requests. We are giving our assent to everything we have prayed. We are committing ourselves to fulfilling a promise—to establish God's kingdom and do his will, to give and forgive, to resist evil in this world—in the years ahead. We will do what we have prayed. That will not always be easy, but in keeping this promise there will be blessing.

Though the Prayer of Jesus reminds us of our brothers and sisters and our responsibility for the world, it remains a prayer addressed to God. When we speak these words, we are telling our Father of our willingness to be partners with God. We are uniting our will with the will of God. The church has been described as the "bride of Christ" because we are seeking to be one with God.

When I was in college, I ran across a small book entitled *The Practice of the Presence of God*. It contained the collected letters of Brother Lawrence of the Resurrection, a seventeenth-century monk who spent most of his life working in the monastery kitchen. He made prayer sound like such joy. He wrote:

Having found in many books different methods of going to God, and diverse practices of the spiritual life, I thought this would serve rather to puzzle me than facilitate what I sought after, which was nothing but how to become wholly God's.

This made me resolve to give all for the all . . . and I began to live as if there was none but He and I in the world.[1]

He went on to describe a relationship with God of which I was immediately envious. It had all the characteristics of the deepest friendship and most abiding love. I too resolved to give my all for the all. I did not take a vow that day, but in the years since I've discovered what that vow should be. It should be the Prayer of Jesus.

Next time you are praying like Jesus, imagine yourself standing before an altar. God is standing with you, and for that moment, there is no one but you and God in this world. You hear these words spoken:

Our Father, who art in heaven,
hallowed be thy name.
Thy kingdom come. Thy will be done,
on earth as it is in heaven.
Give us this day our daily bread.
Forgive us our sins,
as we forgive those who sin against us.
Lead us not into temptation,
but deliver us from evil.
For thine is the kingdom
and the power and the glory forever.

What will you say? I hope you will respond with, "Amen." Remember, you are not the only one taking that vow. God is also standing at that altar. God has also listened to those words. God has promised to deliver you from evil and lead you from temptation. God has vowed to forgive your sins and give you all you need. God has chosen you as his partner in bringing about his kingdom. You are his beloved. You are not the only one saying, "Amen."

On that day when every man and every woman takes this vow, the words of prophecy will come true. "Now the dwelling of God is with men, and he will live with them. They will be his people, and God himself will be with them and be their God. He will wipe every tear from their eyes. There will be no more death or mourning or crying or pain, for the old order of things has passed away" (Rev. 21:3–4).

Amen.

---

1. Brother Lawrence, *The Practice of the Presence of God* (Revell, 1958), p. 31. This classic of practical Christian devotion should be required reading for Christians. It explains what the Bible means by "praying continually."